THE FILMS OF
ALFRED HITCHCOCK

THE FILMS OF
ALFRED HITCHCOCK

NEIL SINYARD

GALLERY BOOKS
An Imprint of W. H. Smith Publishers Inc.
112 Madison Avenue
New York City 10016

This book was devised and produced by
Multimedia Books Ltd.

Editor: Richard Rosenfeld
Production: Karen Bromley
Design: Roger Kohn
Picture Research: David Sutherland

First published in the United States of America 1989 by
Gallery Books, an imprint of W. H. Smith Publishers Inc.,
112 Madison Avenue, New York, NY 10016.

ISBN 0 8317 3321 0

Typeset by Rapidset and Design Ltd.
Origination by BTA Reprographics Ltd.
Printed in Italy by Imago Publishing

Endpapers: *The biplane chasing
Cary Grant in* **North by
Northwest** *(1959) crashes into a
passing truck, leaving Grant free
to track down his assailants.*

Page 1: *A deadpan Alfred
Hitchcock on the set of* **Psycho**
*(1960). The lighting cameraman,
John L. Russell, worked on
Hitchcock's television series, and
was hired for* **Psycho** *to speed up
the amount of time spent shooting
the film. Every other Hitchcock
movie between 1951 and 1964
was photographed by Hitchcock's
regular associate, Robert Burks.*

Pages 2-3: *Hitchcock
concentrating on a scene from*
Frenzy *(1972). This was his first
film in England for over twenty
years following his move to the US
in 1939.*

This page: *The figure in the water
is a dummy, a joke on the first
corpse in* **Frenzy** *(1972).
It illustrates both Hitchcock's flair
for publicity and his macabre
sense of humor.*

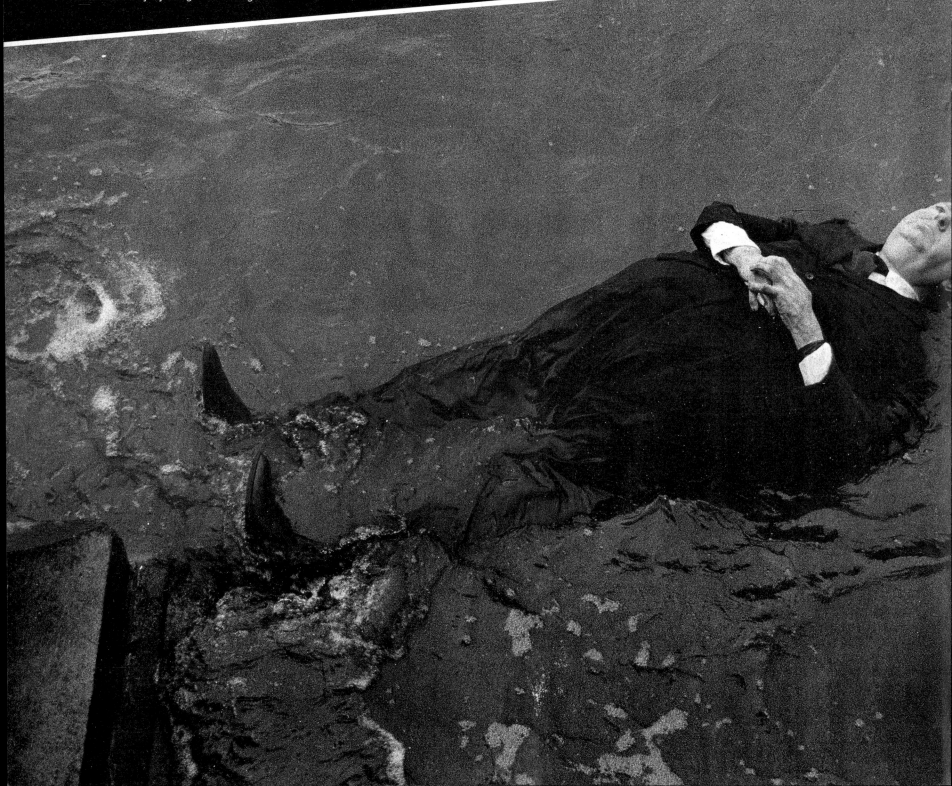

CONTENTS

INTRODUCTION

Asked on one occasion what he would like on his headstone, Alfred Hitchcock replied: "This is what we do to bad little boys." When he died in April 1980, the tributes were very different from that. He was, quite simply, the Master of Suspense.

To Hitchcock, suspense in cinema primarily meant emotion. He distinguished suspense from surprise, which was sudden shock, and from mystery, which was an intellectual puzzle. Suspense meant a prolongation of fear, expectation and desire. "Suspense is like a woman," he said, "the more left to the imagination, the more the excitement." But his primary aim was to move, stimulate and involve the audience. Everything in his films – the use of subjective camerawork, the casting of glamorous stars, the violence of his images – was directed towards that end. "Ours not to reason why," he said, "ours just to scare the hell out of people." In classics like **Psycho** (1960) and **The Birds** (1963), he did that better than anyone.

This book traces the development whereby Hitchcock became the master of suspense and established a unique rapport with cinema audiences. It follows his evolution from the exhilarating escapism of his English classics like **The 39 Steps** (1935) and **The Lady Vanishes** (1938) to the pessimism and passion of Hollywood masterpieces like **Shadow of a Doubt** (1943) and **Vertigo** (1958). In so doing, it recalls some of the most memorable moments in movie history. In the shadows of this argument lurks another intriguing question: was there anything in Hitchcock's life or personality to account for the murderous preoccupations of his movies?

On the surface, there is nothing in the least mysterious or disquieting about Hitchcock's life. Born in London in 1899, the son of a poulterer and greengrocer, he was educated at a Jesuit school, St Ignatius College, and, by all accounts, was a quiet, reserved child.

He was also a keen filmgoer. When he later read that an American company, Famous Players-Lasky, were going into production at Islington, he applied for a job and was employed as a title designer. By stages he worked up to the position of director.

In 1926, he married Alma Reville, a writer and editor who was to be an indispensable support throughout his career. The marriage endured until his death. Their daughter, Patricia, had a brief acting career before her marriage, appearing in three Hitchcock films (**Stage Fright**, 1950, **Strangers on a Train**, 1951, and **Psycho**). Outside of movies, Hitchcock listed his interests as home, garden and a few paintings. "We live a very suburban life here," Hitchcock said. "We're in bed by nine o'clock every night."

Childhood trauma

Yet a few anxieties ruffle the surface of this ostensibly ordered life. For example, there is the famous story how, at the age of five, Hitchcock was locked in a police cell for a few minutes as a practical joke by a friend of his father. Doubt has been cast on whether the incident actually happened, but that only raises the question: why then did Hitchcock constantly refer to it as if it had? It must either have triggered a nightmare or answered some sort of need for one. Certainly the fear of authority, of wrongful arrest and the irrational feelings of guilt which the incident apparently stirred in Hitchcock, are all feelings that recur powerfully in his movies.

Similar implications might be drawn from Hitchcock's educational background. He merely said that the Jesuit College taught him the value of discipline, but might not such a strict upbringing lead to a residue of repression that could only be released in the tense, cathartic romanticism of his uniquely personal cinema? This particularly applies to his American films, for America seems to have had an enormous effect on Hitchcock, opening up a more profound perception of life's potential tragedy and a painful, searching insight into the varieties of sexual desire.

This is not to argue that Hitchcock's work is steeped in anguished autobiography, but merely to say that he might have been more deeply involved in his material than he cared to admit. His movies, as much as those of any other director, seem to bring the film-maker's unconscious tantalizingly close to the surface. Hitchcock's films sometimes take the form of a physical journey which corresponds to the inner progress and development of a main character. It is hoped that this journey through Hitchcock's career will have something of the same effect, and that it will reveal there was even more to the man and the films than meets the eye. As a trailer, perhaps one might cite a classic Hitchcock understatement, another epitaph of a kind, whose wit has a decidedly sinister ring: "I have brought murder back into the home – where it belongs."

◄ *Hitchcock caught between shots for his thriller about the Cuban missile crisis,* **Topaz** *(1969), based on the novel by Leon Uris.*

▲ *Hitchcock directing Paul Newman in a scene from his Cold War thriller,* **Torn Curtain** *(1966). This was Hitch's last working association with a big Hollywood star and was not one of his happiest. One biographer has suggested that Newman offended the great director at a dinner party by preferring beer to his host's vintage wine. Newman's version is that he was promised the film script would be improved but that it never was. Perhaps the real reason for their difficult relationship is that Hitchcock was unhappy working with Method actors–as far as he was concerned, the actor's task was not to probe the motivations of his character but to flesh out the visual conception of the director.*

THE ENGLISH HITCHCOCK (1925-1939)

Between his directing debut in 1925 and the time when he left for Hollywood in 1939, Alfred Hitchcock directed a total of twenty-three films. Surprisingly, in addition to thrillers, these films included rural and musical comedies, offbeat romantic melodramas and faithful adaptations of the work of writers as diverse as Ivor Novello, Noel Coward, Sean O'Casey and John Galsworthy. In his first fifteen years in the film industry in Britain, Hitchcock explored more variety of subject matter than he later attempted in the forty years in Hollywood.

Different conclusions have been drawn from this. Some observers value Hitchcock's British period precisely because it demonstrates his versatility. However, most see it as a period in which, through a process of trial and error, Hitchcock was gradually discovering the particular area in which he excelled. To the charge that it was a limited specialization, he might well have quoted Chopin's reply to those critics who wanted him to write opera rather than exquisite nocturnes: "My kingdom is a small one, but I am king there." Hitchcock came to realize that the thriller was a marvelously flexible form in which to examine what major artists of all the dramatic arts have found infinitely fascinating: the behavior of characters under stress.

Silent classics

Although the Hollywood films are indisputably richer and more consistent in achievement, Hitchcock's work in Britain is of considerable interest. For one thing, it produced some films – **Blackmail** (1929), **Rich and Strange** (1932), **Sabotage** (1936) – that are comparable in quality to his finest American work. Also, it is interesting historically because it straddled the period which saw the transition from silents to talkies. Indeed, **Blackmail** was the first British sound film.

Generally speaking, although some of Hitchcock's silent films,

◄ *Enshrouded by Scotch mist, Madeleine Carroll and Robert Donat escape from their spy captors in* **The 39 Steps** *(1935). The heroine has previously been highly sceptical about the hero's protestations of innocence: she is now beginning to wonder if she was wrong.*

▲ *A production shot from the first British talkie,* **Blackmail** *(1929). The young Hitchcock is checking on his earphones that his Czech leading actress, Anny Ondra, can speak sufficiently good English to be understood. As* *it turned out, she couldn't and her lines had to be dubbed in by Joan Barry. Sound recording was in its primitive stages at this time, with the loudly clicking camera for the dialogue scenes being kept in an airless, soundproofed booth.*

like **The Lodger** (1926-27), **The Ring** (1927) and **The Manxman** (1929) are fine achievements, they are not as important in a consideration of his whole body of work as are the silent films of, for example, Fritz Lang in his. Nevertheless, they are the only British silents to command a place in the repertory of classic cinema. Also, although Hitchcock welcomed the coming of sound, it did not fundamentally change his method. While sound was a useful dramatic and expressive tool, it did not alter what he saw as the primary requisite of film direction: "to charge the screen rectangle with emotion". It is hard instantly to call to mind great dialogue scenes in Hitchcock, but any amount of memorable images immediately suggest themselves.

Stylish debut

After various jobs in the film industry, including title designer and writer, Hitchcock came to the attention of the producer Michael Balcon. Knowing of Hitchcock's directing ambitions (he had already begun directing a comedy about Cockney lowlife, **Number Thirteen**, in 1922, but money had run out and the project had been abandoned), Balcon gave the young man his chance.

Because of an agreement between Balcon and Erich Pommer, the head of the UFA studios in Berlin, Hitchcock's first two films were made in Germany. **The Pleasure Garden** (1925-27) concerned the friendship between two chorus girls and their different involvement with two colonial men, one of whom later reveals himself to be an adulterer and killer. It was a stylish debut and attracted the attention of the critics. In Balcon's words, "Hitch the director was in business." This was followed by **The Mountain Eagle** (1926-27) about a village schoolmistress pursued by a shop manager. When she seeks refuge in the mountains, she meets a mysterious recluse whom she later marries. "A very bad picture," was Hitchcock's own verdict, and it is now believed to be lost.

Most Germanic film

Hitchcock's sojourn in Germany gave him the opportunity to see films by masters like Fritz Lang and F. W. Murnau. Their influence is evident in his next and most Germanic film, **The Lodger** (1926-27), although it was his first to be wholly set and shot in England. It was also his first suspense thriller. This "story of the London fog" is about a lodger (Ivor Novello) whose suspicious behavior causes fellow tenants to suspect him of being Jack the Ripper. For scenes in which the tenants hear the suspect pace the floor, Hitchcock built a glass ceiling so that the man could be seen from below, walking up and down in his room. Eventually he is found to be guiltless, but not before he has been handcuffed and almost lynched by a mob. Hitchcock also contrived a parallel with Christ's crucifixion in a scene where the people try to lift him and his arms are tied together. Years later in **I Confess** (1953), a similar feeling is evoked when a priest is reviled by an angry mob.

Page 10: *Three images of Ivor Novello as* **The Lodger** *(1926-27).*
Left: *Ivor Novello in a tensely composed shot, evoking the horror films of German Expressionism. Novello is a prototype of a number of subsequent Hitchcock leading men: dark, handsome, suggesting turbulent psychological depths and hinting at murderous melancholy.*

Center: *Ivor Novello's anxiously pacing image is seen through a thick plate-glass ceiling while his listening landlady begins to suspect that he might be Jack the Ripper. This shot is a brilliant example of visuals implying the existence of sound in the silent cinema. The scene's visual extravagance shows the influence on Hitchcock of the German Expressionist silent cinema.*

Right: *Hitchcock called this film the "first true Hitchcock movie". Novello's pose – arms raised, handcuffed to a railing - evokes the Crucifixion. This was Hitchcock's first film treatment of the "wrong man" theme to which he returned obsessively in later films. "The theme of the innocent man being accused provides the audience with a greater sense of danger," he once said. "It's easier for them to identify with him than a guilty man on the run."*

◄ *Levett (Miles Mander) being seduced by a native girl (Nita Naldi) in a passionate scene from Hitchcock's first completed film as director,* **The Pleasure Garden** *(1925-27). His ensnarement leads to moral degeneration and murder.*

▲ *A dramatic shot of Hitchcock (foreground) directing a scene from* **The Mountain Eagle** *(1926) at the Emelka studio in Munich. This was one of the two films he made in Germany at the start of his directing career. Behind him in rapt concentration is his assistant, Alma Reville. Hitchcock and Alma were married later in 1926; she remained his most valued adviser until his death in 1980.*

11

The Lodger draws on the style of German Expressionism with its sinister play of light and shade. Its harsh portrait of mob violence and moral righteousness also anticipates similar themes and portraiture that will occur in German classic films during the rise of Nazism, notably in Fritz Lang's **M** (1931) and **The Testament of Dr Mabuse** (1933). Hitchcock's style was always a subtle blend of behavioral realism and a visually Expressionist anguish and exaggeration. In Truffaut's words, "Hitchcock loathed the ordinary." The film is weakened by its upbeat ending. There seems a conflict of presentation between the sinister behavior of the main character and the necessity to redeem him because he is played by a star actor.

Even so, its tension and bold technique are positive indications of the greatness that was to come, and the theme of an innocent man being hounded as if he were guilty became a Hitchcock obsession. It was also the start of Hitchcock's practice of appearing in his own films – in **The Lodger**, apparently, "simply to fill the screen". ("Later it became a superstition," Hitchcock would say, "and then a gag.") The distributor had considerable doubts about the film, finding it turgid and heavy-handed, but Balcon arranged a screening for the press, who were extremely enthusiastic and it became a big hit.

Degradation

Hitchcock's next film was **Downhill** (1927), again starring Novello and based on a play which Novello had co-written. The title proved sadly prophetic for, although it had its inventive moments, it failed to continue the promise of **The Lodger**. Out of loyalty to a childhood pact, a young man (Ivor Novello) chivalrously takes the blame for an offence his friend has committed and is expelled from school. (One of the intertitles at this point in the film has since become something of a collector's item: "Does that mean, sir, that I won't be able to play for the Old Boys?") He subsequently drifts into a series of disasters and winds up as a gigolo.

Quite a lot of future Hitchcock is bubbling under the surface of that material – transference of guilt, seedy sexuality, the theme of degradation. The film also includes Hitchcock's first dream sequence, to convey the young man's hallucinatory sense of humiliation. The situation of the ex-public schoolboy down and out in Paris has an intriguing pre-Orwellian flavor, but the acting is weak, the ending sentimental, and the dialogue (in Hitchcock's blunt description) "dreadful".

The film which followed, an adaptation of Noel Coward's **Easy Virtue** (1927), starred Isabel Jeans as a notorious rich girl who has divorced her drunken husband and caused the suicide of a man

Downhill *(1927).*
▲ *Isabel Jeans with Hannah Jones (left) and ◄ with Ivor Novello.*
The film is based on a play co-written by Ivor Novello and concerns the moral degeneration of a public schoolboy after he has been unjustly expelled for protecting a friend. Isabel Jeans plays an actress who represents one stage on the hero's road to ruin: the shot above suggests the decadent atmosphere into which the hero sinks.

The critics and public were generally disappointed by the film after the success of the thriller **The Lodger,** *(1926-27), but in this film Hitchcock was more interested in satire and style.*

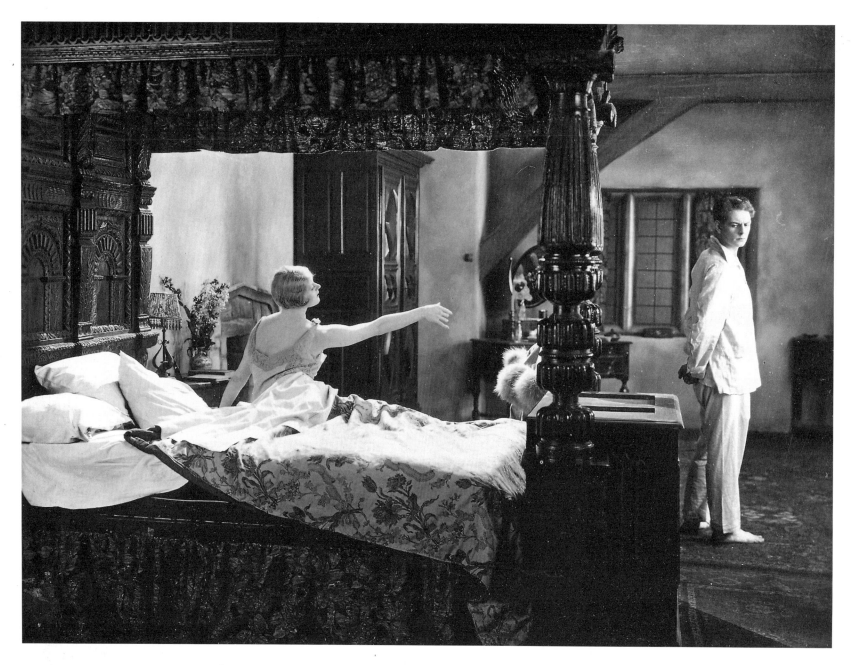

who loved her. She marries a gentleman (Robin Irvine) who knows nothing of her past, but his family's hostility towards the girl leads to the mother discovering the truth about her and compelling the son to divorce her. The film has some imaginative touches. For instance, the heroine's acceptance of the gentleman's marriage proposal is shown entirely through the reaction of an eavesdropping switchboard operator. But a silent adaptation of any Noel Coward play seems doomed before it begins. The unsuitability of these last two projects prompted Hitchcock to escape from the benevolent paternalism of Michael Balcon and join British International Pictures (BIP) at Elstree.

Best of the silents

His first work for BIP, **The Ring** (1927), is probably the best of his silent films. It is the story of two boxers (Carl Brisson and Ian Hunter) involved with the same girl (Lillian Hall Davis). The title stands not only for the boxing ring, but for the wedding ring which one of them puts on the girl's finger, and for the bracelet (sometimes flaunted, sometimes hidden) that is a gift from the other man and symbolizes her adultery. The story's movement from fairground booths to the Albert Hall allows Hitchcock the opportunity

▲ *Isabel Jeans and Robert Irvine in an expressive moment from* **Easy Virtue** *(1927), Hitchcock's adaption of a play by Noel Coward. A husband has just found out about his wife's past, and is now being pressurized by his family to divorce her. The images from both* **Downhill** *(1927) and* **Easy Virtue** *suggest a tantalizing sexuality that is strongly characteristic of Hitchcock's films.*

▶ *Gordon Harker (left), Carl Brisson (center) and Harry Terry (right) in the opening fairground scene from* **The Ring** *(1927). "One Round Jack", played by Brisson, is so called because he knocks out his opponents in the first round. However he is less successful in dealing with a boxing champion who becomes a rival for his wife's affections.*

for comic social observation. It is more convincing, more real, than anything he had previously attempted. But the main impression remains that of Hitchcock's increasing confidence and economy as a film-maker. This is evidenced in such details as the superimposition of an opponent's face on the hero's punchbag as he practises, or the moment when – at a champagne party – the hero realizes that his wife is with the other man and his mood is conveyed by a shot of his flat champagne. It is a straight human drama, well told and acted.

Hitchcock's next three films were all in a completely different vein, part of the unpredictable pattern of the director's talent and themes around this time. **The Farmer's Wife** (1928) is a rural comedy about the search of a widower (Jameson Thomas) for a wife. Hitchcock makes cruel fun of some of the contenders, and a formal tea party that is reduced to chaos shows his unexpected gift for slapstick comedy. But rusticity and charm were never Hitchcock's cinematic strong suits, and the farmer's choice of his faithful housekeeper (Lillian Hall Davis), who has always adored him, is nothing if not predictable.

Champagne (1928) concerns an heiress who, tricked into believing that her father has gone broke, is reduced to working as a waitress in a nightclub. The theme is not dissimilar to the earlier **Downhill.** Both have uncomfortable portraits of oppressive parenthood – which will be a leitmotif of a number of important Hitchcock films. Generally, however, **Champagne** invites the obvious comment: it lacks sparkle.

Champagne (1928).
◀ In this striking moment the quarreling pair in the foreground (Jean Bradin, left, and Betty Balfour, right) is contrasted with the romantic couples in the background. The early scenes of **Champagne** are quite sharp evocations of privilege, wealth, wilful romanticism and the hedonism of the 1920s, but the film soon falls flat.

▼ Betty Balfour (center) plays a millionaire's daughter tricked into believing that her fortune has vanished, and compelled to find a job. Applying for work in a photo agency, she experiences for the first time the humiliation and exploitation of the poor as the boss's sleazy aide lifts up her skirt with his shoe.

Blackmail *(1929).*
▼ *The murder scene. A frivolous flirtation leads to attempted rape and murder in self-defense. Alice (Anny Ondra) looks down at the bread knife, a domestic object transformed into a weapon. The shadow of the knife on her dress, like a bloodstain, anticipates her forthcoming obsession with the murder weapon.*

▶ *The dramatic poster seems as excited about the coming of talkies as about the actual story. Yet Hitchcock was not so interested in dialogue ("our mother tongue as it should be-spoken") as in the visuals.*

Tortured heroines

Hitchcock's next film, **The Manxman** (1929), was in a different category of achievement. A fisherman (Carl Brisson) and a lawyer (Malcolm Keen) have been friends since youth and both love the same girl (Anny Ondra). The gauche fisherman asks the lawyer to propose to the girl on his behalf, but is rejected because of her father's opposition to his lowly status. While the fisherman is away making his fortune, the lawyer pursues the girl. When they hear that the fisherman is dead, they become lovers. However, he returns; he and the girl marry, and she bears a child whose father is actually the lawyer. But when she suggests to the lawyer that they run away together, he rebuffs her, for such a scandal would ruin his promising legal career. She attempts suicide, and appears for her crime before her lover, now a judge. Finally, he acknowledges his responsibility for her and the baby.

The themes of guilt and thwarted love anticipate **Under Capricorn** (1949). And the situation of the heroine tortured and trapped between two men, one blind, the other selfish, looks ahead to **Notorious** (1946). With its location shooting, where wild seas and oppressive cliffs are used to heighten mood and intensify atmosphere, **The Manxman** has something of the fervor of D. W. Griffith's melodramas. But its release was delayed and Hitchcock never seemed to feel very positively about the film. "The only point of interest about that movie is that it was my last silent one," he said.

Exploiting sound

His first thriller since **The Lodger**, **Blackmail** was begun as a silent but, taking note of the popularity of talkies, Hitchcock decided midway through to reshoot some scenes with dialogue. He also added sound effects to some of the sequences already shot. Introducing sound necessitated the dubbing of his Polish-born Czech leading actress, Anny Ondra, whose English was not good. She mouthed her lines while, out of camera range, her understudy Joan Barry spoke them into the microphone.

Technically Hitchcock's most advanced film up to that time, it is also thematically his most interesting. A young lady (Anny Ondra) has an argument with her detective boyfriend (John Longden) and is picked up by an artist (Cyril Ritchard) who invites her back to his studio. There he attempts to rape her and she stabs him to death. A glove she has left at the scene of the crime is found by her detective boyfriend who is investigating this case. She was also seen entering the artist's studio by a man who begins to blackmail her.

It is fascinating to see how Hitchcock adjusted to the new toy of sound. He instantly began to exploit its dramatic possibilities. After the murder, the heroine roams the London streets and comes across a tramp lying in a doorway, his hand dangling limply like that of the man she murdered. As she opens her mouth to scream, Hitchcock cuts to the landlady's screams as she discovers the dead artist. The cut both advances the plot and serves as an extension of the heroine's *imagination* of future discovery. This subjectivity of sound is carried further in a famous scene when a neighbor starts talking about the murder. The word "knife" keeps stabbing through the blur of conversation, pressing unbearably on the heroine's stretched, guilty nerves.

According to Hitchcock, the film was somewhat compromised. He had planned it as a carefully structured piece around the theme of love and duty. It was to open with an illustration of the "duty" theme, showing police arresting a suspect. As the film develops, the

▲ *Paying the price of seduction in* **Blackmail** *(1929). The artist (Cyril Ritchard) is stabbed, and death, in the convention of classic cinema, is signified by the outstretched hand stiffening.*

detective's sense of duty would be compromised by his desire to protect his girlfriend and love would seem to be taking precedence. But the girl would finally be arrested, and the duty theme would resurface. Hitchcock's original ending was to have the detective being asked, "Are you seeing your girl tonight?" and his sad reply: "No, not tonight."

However, for commercial reasons, this was felt to be too depressing. In the finished film, suspicion falls on the blackmailer and, in a chase across the roofs of the British Museum, he falls to his death. For the police, this accident closes the case. This change has damaging effects on the film. Although the British Museum chase is extremely well done, with Hitchcock pointing a contrast between the chaos of the chase and the orderly facade and routine of the Museum – in much the same way as he was to use Mount Rushmore in **North by Northwest** (1959) – the sequence seems a rather arbitrary addition. Also, by changing the ending, the film makes the emphasis on the arrest at the beginning rather pointless.

Curiously, though, the changes do deepen the emotional complexities of the film. Without deserving the violence she provokes, the heroine has behaved coquettishly at the artist's studio. She must be considered partly responsible for his arousal, and hence her murder of him in self-defense is not an untainted act. Desiring to confess, she is dissuaded by her boyfriend when the blackmailer's fate becomes known – another death for which she is indirectly responsible. She is left with an uncomfortable residue of unexpiated guilt. At the end the heroine is shocked by the appearance in the police station of a painting of a laughing but sinister-looking jester that she recognizes from the artist's studio. It rekindles her anguish and the feeling is that, although she is free, it is the artist who might yet have the last laugh.

Anticlimax

The films Hitchcock made in the four years after **Blackmail** were something of an anticlimax. **Juno and the Paycock** (1930) and **The Skin Game** (1931) were adapted from plays by Sean O'Casey and John Galsworthy respectively. In the former, Hitchcock had a good cast (Sara Allgood as Juno, Edward Chapman as the dreamy husband, John Laurie as the son who is shot by Sinn Fein as an informer). The film was kindly received by the press and by O'Casey. But Hitchcock always professed himself embarrassed by this enthusiasm: to him, the film had no cinematic interest.

The same could be said for his stolid adaptation of Galsworthy's play, about the clash of values between a decaying aristocratic conservatism and the middle-class materialism that is taking its place. The performances of C. V. France as the conservative landowner Hillcrest, and Edmund Gwenn as the thrusting industrialist Hornblower, stand up reasonably well, but it is talkative without saying anything and Hitchcock cannot bring it to life.

His only thriller during this period was **Murder!** (1930), based on a story by Clemence Dane and Helen Simpson (who wrote **Under Capricorn**) and one of Hitchcock's few whodunnits. Herbert Marshall plays a grand actor of the old school. As a member of a jury that has convicted an actress of murder, he begins to have doubts and becomes an amateur sleuth in order to unmask the actual killer. Hitchcock clearly enjoys the theatrical background of the story and it is the kind of setting to which he will return. He also obviously enjoys material that undermines the complacent notion of the infallibility of legal justice. The film is equally interesting for

▶ *An attempted suicide in **The Skin Game** (1931), Hitchcock's lackluster adaptation of a play by John Galsworthy.*

▼ *Norah Baring plays an actress accused of murder in **Murder!** (1930). Hitchcock only rarely made such whodunnits, preferring suspense to surprise. **Murder!** features one of his favorite dramatic backgrounds, the world of the theater. The film's striking use of shadow and lighting prompted the French critics Eric Rohmèr and Claude Chabrol to compare the film's style with German Expressionism and particularly with the work of F. W. Murnau, the director of **Nosferatu** (1922).*

its bold use of interior monologue, its subjective camera-work, and its bizarre sexuality (the murderer turns out to be a transvestite trapeze artist).

One feels that **Number Seventeen** (1932) could have been a thriller had not Hitchcock got carried away by technique. The first part is a sort of parody of the Old Dark House style of horror film. A detective and a tramp in a deserted house stumble upon a gang of jewel thieves. One of these is a girl who stays mute for two-thirds of the film for no other reason than to provoke a laugh when she suddenly starts talking ("I'm not really dumb – it was just a crook's trick"). The second half of the film is preoccupied with a mad chase between a goods train and a Green Line bus which ultimately collide with and sink a cross-Channel ferry. It looks exactly what it is: a chase between a toy coach and a model electric train, filmed by Hitchcock with childlike exuberance and not a great deal of point.

▲ *John Stuart and Anne Grey are spooked by the Old Dark House in* **Number Seventeen** *(1932), Hitchcock's absurd parody of the horror film. Most of the action occurs on the staircase and the landing, where an assortment of English eccentrics keep colliding.*

Inner demons

One of Hitchcock's favorites among his British films was **Rich and Strange** (1932), and it is still one of the most interesting films of his career. A suburban married couple (Henry Kendall and Joan Barry), bored with their lives and each other, unexpectedly inherit some money and go on a world cruise in an endeavor to revive their marriage. Various adventures ensue: a costume party; extra-marital affairs, in which the wife is courted by an English gentleman and her husband is seduced and robbed by a phoney princess. Finally, there is a shipwreck, from which they are rescued and fed by a junkload of Chinese pirates and then discover that they have just been eating the ship's cat. They return to their humdrum lives, sadder but not much wiser.

The satire on commuter life and on the theme of innocents

▼ *The fancy-dress ball aboard ship in* **Rich and Strange** *(1932), worlds away from the boredom of suburbia. In this intoxicating atmosphere Henry Kendall is attracted to a princess (Betty Amann, standing) who turns out to be a phoney. His wife (Joan Barry) looks on impassively: she too soon has a fling.*

74-144

◀ *Joan Barry and Henry Kendall as the bickering married couple in* **Rich and Strange** *(1932), entitled* **East of Shanghai** *in the USA. Here their ship is wrecked but they can't escape because the cabin door is stuck: the prospect of imminent death concentrates their minds wonderfully, and they declare their love for each other. The title, incidentally, is taken from Shakespeare's* The Tempest, *another tale of shipwreck and emotional growth:*

    Full fathom five thy father lies;
    Of his bones are coral made;
    Those are pearls that were his eyes;
    Nothing of him that doth fade
    But doth suffer a sea-change
    Into something rich and strange.

abroad is well done, but it is the increasing strangeness of events and tone that is most striking. The theme of the film has been well summarized by the critic Robin Wood: "bourgeois normality is empty and unsatisfing, everything beyond it is terrifying".

Hitchcock returned to this theme with supreme profundity and power in **Shadow of a Doubt** (1943), and it was a shadow theme running throughout his work, and possibly even his life. (Would it be too fanciful to suggest that, for Hitchcock, making films about murder was a way of escaping the dissatisfactions of bourgeois normality and taming his own inner demons?) It is clear the film was deeply felt and Hitchcock was depressed by its abject commercial failure, which he blamed on himself for not casting stronger principals. He was not to make another film quite like **Rich and Strange**.

A brief musical interlude

Although he did direct a brief linking contribution to a 1930 British musical **Elstree Calling**, basically a compilation of variety acts from the likes of Jack Hulbert, Cicely Courtneidge and Anna May Wong, Hitchcock's only full-length musical was **Waltzes from Vienna** (1933). This was a story about Johann Strauss the Elder and his son. Hitchcock was not to make another film quite like this one either, for which we can feel profoundly grateful. Hitchcock described it as his "lowest ebb".

It has some spirited moments of comic understatement, like the query of the servant after being kicked downstairs: "Will that be all, sir?" But, within two weeks of shooting commencing Hitchcock assembled his cast together, including stars Jessie Matthews, Fay

Compton and Edmund Gwenn, and told them all mournfully: "I hate this sort of stuff. Melodrama is the only thing I can do." Fortunately, he was entering into a period when he showed that, if suspense melodrama was the only thing he could do, he could do it better than anyone else.

Thrilled to death

The six films Hitchcock made between 1934 and 1938 set the seal on his reputation. They are all thrillers, with a hefty leavening of comedy in most of them, and they are all escapist in tone. "I am out to give the public good, healthy mental shake ups," Hitchcock said at this time. "Civilization has become so screening and sheltering that we cannot experience sufficient thrills at first hand. Therefore to prevent ourselves becoming sluggish and jellified, we have to experience them artificially."

Hitchcock's advocacy of the invigorating effects of a liberal dose of melodrama stands in contrast not only to the realist sobriety of the British documentary film which was then developing strongly, but also in contrast to the mood of the times. His motives sometimes allude to the anxieties of what the poet W. H. Auden has described as a "low dishonest decade". The politics of terrorism surface in **The Man Who Knew Too Much** (1934) and **Sabotage** (1936). International espionage is afoot in **The 39 Steps** (1935) and **Secret Agent** (1936). And **The Lady Vanishes** (1938) can be seen as an allegory about the condition of England on the eve of world war.

In this classic movie a group of disparate and desperate English people band together against a foreign foe, and an appeaser waving a white handkerchief in surrender (Prime Minister Neville Chamberlain waving his Munich peace pact?) is shot for his pains.

However, poverty and politics, two of the great issues of the 1930s, are both peripheral in these films. What they delight in most are the techniques of good storytelling, the excitement of the double chase, the banter and battle between the sexes, and a very English fascination with murder. "The English for some reason seem to have more bizarre murders than any other country," Hitchcock once observed. Perhaps this is because the English overlay of repression and restraint in the national character becomes twisted in bizarre directions when these boundaries are breached. Some fine British writers – Wilkie Collins, Sir Arthur Conan Doyle, John Buchan, Emlyn Williams, G. K. Chesterton – found the outlet for their potential dark side in writing crime fiction. Notably inhibited and reserved, Hitchcock found his outlet for his suppressed self in becoming the Master of Suspense.

Reunion with Balcon

The first in Hitchcock's thriller sextet of the mid-1930s was **The Man Who Knew Too Much** (1934). It was also a reunion with Michael Balcon, by then head of production at Gaumont British. An English couple (Leslie Banks and Edna Best) on holiday in Switzerland witness the killing of a secret agent (Pierre Fresnay) after he

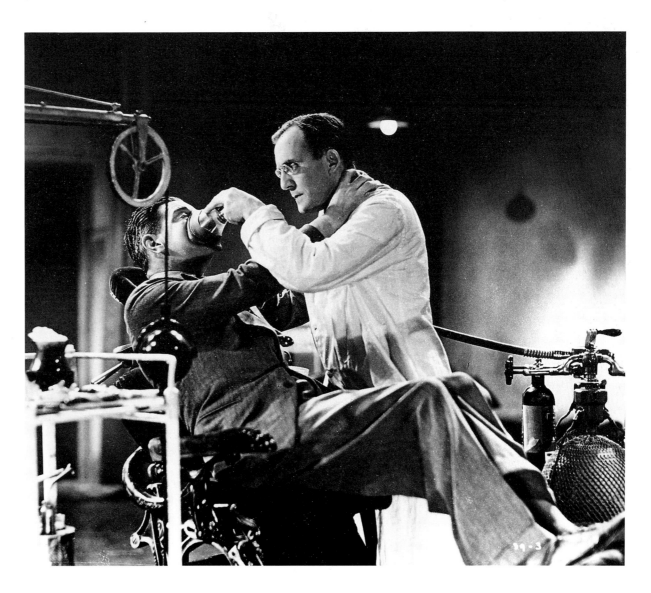

► *Leslie Banks' search for his kidnapped daughter leads him to the dentist's chair in* **The Man Who Knew Too Much** *(1934).*

has managed to tell them of an impending political assassination to take place in London. Their daughter (Nova Pilbeam) is kidnapped to keep them quiet, but the assassination attempt at the Royal Albert Hall is foiled when the wife screams at the crucial moment in the concert. The villains are finally smoked out in a shoot-out modeled closely on the famous siege at Sydney Street in 1911.

Hitchcock was to remake the film in America in 1955-6 with more gloss and more depth. This 1934 version has as much comedy as tension. The Royal Albert Hall sequence is a virtuoso piece of direction, though a measure of Hitchcock's maturity is that, in the later version, he does not repeat the mistake of dissipating tension by cutting from the concert to shots of the villains listening in on the radio. The final shoot-out in the original version is a bit of a bore, and the film's most durable contribution remains Peter Lorre's colorful performance as the villain. But its lightness, wit and pace made it enormously successful.

▲ *A moment from the final shoot-out in* **The Man Who Knew Too Much** *(1934). This scene was based on the 1911 Siege of Sydney Street, when a group of foreign anarchists exchanged fire with the police and army rather than surrender. The scene was dropped from Hitchcock's remake of the story in 1956.*

Political intrigue

Hitchcock followed it with **The 39 Steps** (1935), perhaps the most famous and acclaimed of his British films and one of the best thrillers of the decade. Some purists were upset by its radical departure from John Buchan's original story, although, intriguingly, Hitchcock always claimed that Buchan was a writer who had a considerable influence on his work. He liked what he called Buchan's "understatement of highly dramatic ideas". Other favored Buchan themes – his interest in the split between appearance and reality, his distrust of the normal, and his fear of "how thin is the protection of civilization" – are identical to those which Hitchcock will pursue throughout his career.

Robert Donat plays Richard Hannay, caught up in a plot of murder and political intrigue when a mysterious female spy (Lucie

The 39 Steps (1935).
▼ *After shooting Mr Memory, Professor Jordan (Godfrey Tearle, center) tries to escape by jumping onto the stage but is quickly surrounded by the police. The distant camera angle makes the melodramatic events seem like a moment from a stage performance, a bizarre production number from a Gilbert and Sullivan operetta.*

Overleaf: *One more river to cross: Donat and Carroll hide from their pursuers in* **The 39 Steps** *(1935). The two are handcuffed together in a mutual antagonism that grows into affection.*

Mannheim) flops across his bed in the middle of the night with a knife in her back. Hannay escapes to Scotland; traces a respected Professor (Godfrey Tearle), who, by holding up his hand to show a missing joint on one of his fingers, reveals himself as the chief villain. Our hero finds himself handcuffed to a lady (Madeleine Carroll) who thinks he is a murderer; and finally traces the secret organization back to the London Palladium.

"I reckoned that two sets of people would be looking for me," Hannay says in the novel after discovering the murder. He means both the killers of the spy and also the police who would suspect him of the murder. This double-hunt structure was to be a favorite ploy of Hitchcock's (**Saboteur**, 1942, **Strangers on a Train**, 1951, and **North by Northwest**, 1959, are three other conspicuous examples). Otherwise Hitchcock's adaptation of Buchan has much of the spirit of the original but little of the substance.

A throwaway reference to Hannay's visit to the music-hall at the beginning of the novel is the only trace of the inspiration for the character of Mr Memory (Wylie Watson), one of the film's most memorable creations and the means by which the villains transport their secrets out of the country.

A brief reference to a Scottish crofter's wife in a later chapter is expanded in the film to one of its finest sequences, when Hannay hides out in the cottage of a farming couple (John Laurie and Peggy Ashcroft). The husband is as jealous and conniving as the wife is meek and kind. Hannay might be handcuffed temporarily to a beautiful lady later in the film, but the cottager's wife is chained to her husband for life. With masterly economy, Hitchcock suggests a tense marriage, an oppressive religious atmosphere and a generosity of spirit in the wife whose gift to Hannay of her husband's overcoat, his prayer book in the breast pocket, later saves Hannay's life by stopping a bullet.

Otherwise the film is memorable for its famous shock cut from a cleaner's screams to a train whistle. There is also the hero's rapid improvisation of a rousing political speech when he blunders into a public meeting; and the saucy humor Hitchcock draws from the situation of a man and woman handcuffed together but more antagonistic than amorous. The poise of the leading performances should be mentioned, as should the brisk and witty script of Hitchcock's favorite screenwriter of this period, Charles Bennett. He had worked on **The Man Who Knew Too Much** and collaborated on the next three films after **The 39 Steps**.

Friend or foe

Hitchcock followed his adaptation of John Buchan with an adaptation of W. Somerset Maugham. **Secret Agent** (1936) is based on two of Maugham's "Ashenden" adventure stories and concerns an Englishman, Ashenden (John Gielgud), who is sent to Switzerland during the First World War to kill an enemy agent. He is accompanied by an apprentice spy (Madeleine Carroll) posing as his wife and by a Mexican double agent (Peter Lorre). Ashenden mistakenly kills an innocent man and it is only on the train home that he realizes the real enemy agent is an American (Robert Young) who has befriended them.

The film failed to repeat the success of **The 39 Steps**. Hitchcock tended to blame John Gielgud's rather languid performance in the leading role for the film's failure. As Hitchcock put it, the audience was unable to identify with "a hero who doesn't want to be a hero and doesn't act like one". In retrospect, this looks like one of the most interesting aspects of the film, and its ironic attitude to guilt and innocence was refined and developed in later projects. It also exploits Hitchcock's fascination with the deception of appearances. A pleasant American turns out to be a dangerous spy, and even a chocolate factory is a center for espionage.

Hitchcock's inventive use of sound is revealed when, in church, the hero hears an organ mysteriously sounding a single note and discovers the grisly explanation: the dead body of an agent slumped over the keys. **Secret Agent** might lack the sparkle of **The 39 Steps**, but its thoughtful anti-heroics and character complications are commendable compensations.

By an odd coincidence, Hitchcock's next film was based on Joseph Conrad's novel, **The Secret Agent**, and retitled **Sabotage** (1936). It begins with the lights going out all over London, an act of sabotage designed to frighten the population but which only succeeds in amusing them. The saboteur is told that it is not enough to make the city laugh, he must terrify the people out of their wits. It is almost a metaphor for Hitchcock's film-making: when the lights go down, it is not enough simply to divert and entertain, he must involve and frighten. The saboteur in the film, Mr Verloc (Oscar Homolka), unlike his counterpart in the novel, is the manager of a cinema.

Unexpected shock

Sabotage is the greatest of Hitchcock's British films, because of the complex sympathy it arouses for all the characters. Although there are many deaths in the film, there are no villains, only victims. The film's biggest shock – it is probably the most effectively unexpected shock in Hitchcock prior to the shower murder in **Psycho** – is the moment when the bomb goes off on the London bus. It kills, among others, Mrs Verloc's scatterbrained young brother (Desmond Tester) who, unsuspectingly, has been carrying the explosive among some cans of film.

"I should never have allowed the bomb to go off," Hitchcock said later. "If you build an audience up to that point the explosion becomes strangely anticlimactic. You work the audience up to such a degree that they need the relief." It is a startling moment because Hitchcock precedes it with a long buildup that intensifies the audience's sympathy with the boy (as he is made fun of at the market and plays happily with a dog on the bus). Nevertheless, without the impact of that sudden irruption of chaos into the characters' lives and into the audience's expectations, it is hard to see how Hitchcock could have got the remainder of the film to work. It does so, triumphantly. What follows is a remarkably sustained stretch of film, beginning with the reaction of Mrs Verloc (Sylvia Sidney) to the news of her brother's death and culminating in her almost involuntary murder of her husband because of his involvement.

Hitchcock visualizes her torment by images of hallucination (her imagining that she sees her brother in a crowd) and moments of painful counterpoint to her distraught mood (the audience's laughter in the cinema at the cartoon "Who Killed Cock Robin?" as she tries to come to terms with the enormity of what has happened).

Sabotage (1936).

▲ *The policeman (John Loder) comforts Mrs Verloc (Sylvia Sidney) after she has murdered her husband. He is proposing that they run away together before her crime is discovered. However, she is still in a state of shock following the death of her brother. The tense composition suggests two people tormented by guilt and confusion.*

▶ *Hitchcock's re-creation of the Lord Mayor's Show, a symbol of a British way of life which the saboteur hopes to undermine. The procession delays the delivery of a bomb hidden inside a can of film, resulting in the unintended killing of the heroine's young brother, who is the unwitting messenger of death.*

The murder is one of the finest scenes Hitchcock had directed up to that point. The conversation between the Verlocs is about cabbage, about the hulking husband's clumsy assurance that things might have been worse ("What would it have been . . . if you had lost me?"). It reveals a marriage based on fondness and companionship more than love. But the subject of the scene is the knife with which the wife carves the meat and to which she is drawn like a magnet. Without anything being said to that end, the husband senses her subconscious intention, rising from the table and coming towards her. Is he trying to save himself, or guiltily offer himself for sacrifice? In a flurry of confused movement, the wife screams, the husband gasps and falls, the knife in his stomach. Only then does the wife utter her first words since the news of the bomb explosion; she simply repeats her brother's name: "Stevie . . . Stevie . . .".

At the script stage, the American actress Sylvia Sidney was understandably perturbed by the absence of dialogue in what was for her the most dramatic section of the film. But, through montage and restrained film acting, Hitchcock conjured up one of her most memorable sequences in movies, and perhaps the best performance of his early British films.

"When a film has been properly staged," Hitchcock later said, "it isn't necessary to rely upon the player's virtuosity or personality for tension and dramatic effects. In my opinion, the chief requisite for an actor is the ability to do nothing well, which is by no means as easy as it sounds. He should be willing to be utilized and wholly integrated into the picture by the director and the camera." This is one of the reasons why Hitchcock's American films seem better acted than his prewar British ones. American actors were better attuned to the film medium, whereas the British actor invariably appeared to be struggling to adapt his theatrical range to the requirements of the film camera. It is also one of the reasons why Hitchcock was in the future to have trouble with Method actors like Montgomery Clift and Paul Newman. They could not adjust to the director's insistence on passivity and neutrality.

Sabotage is not flawless. The role of the detective (John Loder) is weak, and the uneasy resolution of the tale after the murder is lacking in tension. Yet the solidity of the settings and supporting characterizations, the ruthless outrageousness of its plotting, and the ironic and tragic love story that is its core, give the film a profundity and compassion beyond anything else Hitchcock made in this country. It has the grey fatalism and poignant pessimism of a Fritz Lang or Graham Greene.

A lighter theme

As a complete change of mood, Hitchcock then made **Young and Innocent** (1937), in which a struggling writer (Derrick de Marney) is suspected of having murdered a movie star. A policeman's daughter (Nova Pilbeam) becomes involved in the struggle

◀ *In* **Young and Innocent** *(1938), entitled* **The Girl Was Young** *in America, the body of an actress has been found on a Cornish beach. Derrick de Marney* *(second from left) is suspected of her murder; Nova Pilbeam (extreme right) is the young daughter of the chief of police who helps him trace the real culprit.*

to clear his name. It is a light, agreeable film, with some amusing set-pieces (the fugitive blundering into a children's party) and some exciting ones (hero and heroine clinging for their lives in a crumbling mine shaft). The radiant face of the young and innocent heroine, which closes the film and signifies a new phase in the character's life, contrasts tellingly with the close-up with which the film has opened: the face of the raging married actress, immediately before she is killed. The gigolo hero's weirdness is rather charmlessly acted, but Nova Pilbeam gives an attractive performance.

However, all this is secondary to the highlight and real *raison d'être* of the film, which is a single camera movement. Hero and heroine have discovered that the murderer has a twitch in his eyes and are searching for him in a large hotel.

"I place the camera in the highest position, above the hotel lounge, next to the ceiling," said Hitchcock, "and we dolly it down, right through the lobby, into the big ballroom, and past the dancers, the bandstand and the musicians, right up to a close-up of the drummer. The musicians are all in blackface and we stay on the drummer's face until his eyes fill the screen. And then the eyes twitch."

It is not only a masterful example of the camera telling a story, of Hitchcock's careful orchestration of camera movement from general to particular, small to large, detached observation to emotional involvement. At this juncture, the camera becomes a finger of fate, a bird of prey going for the eyes. As he realizes he is being watched, the drummer's guilt begins to surface, his mad cadenzas helplessly drawing attention to himself, cutting a path of chaos across the harmony of the music and disclosing the uncontrollable agitation in his mind that will give him away. This whole last scene transforms the film. If everything had been on that level, **Young and Innocent** would have been a masterpiece.

Bizarre imagery

"Masterpiece" is a word that has sometimes been applied to **The Lady Vanishes** (1938), which is, to some extent, a summation of Hitchcock's British films. Going home to England from a Balkan holiday resort, a young heiress (Margaret Lockwood) strikes up an acquaintance with an old lady on a train (Dame May Whitty). The heiress is disturbed when the old lady not only vanishes but the other passengers deny she ever existed. Only a young collector of folk songs (Michael Redgrave) believes her. Together they discover that the old lady is a British secret agent who has been kidnapped while attempting to smuggle a secret code back to England. After a gun battle between the English people on the train and the foreign agents who are trying to abscond with her, the secrets are safely delivered.

Because of a fine script by Frank Launder and Sidney Gilliat, the film crackles with lively comic invention. Charters (Basil Radford) and Caldicott (Naunton Wayne) are two classic stereotypes of English eccentricity. Their reason for denying the existence of the old lady is simply that any delay while a search is carried out might mean missing the Test Match in England. Michael Redgrave and Margaret Lockwood make a sparkling romantic couple whose antagonistic wisecracks ("My father always said, 'Never desert a lady in trouble' – he took it to the point of marrying my mother") have a wit that rivals that of classic Hollywood screwball comedies of the 1930s.

Hitchcock is in his element, with bizarre imagery that includes a nun in high heels and a fight amid a magician's props. **The Lady Vanishes** might be called one of his most audacious conjuring tricks, in which even a discarded label from a packet of tea can change the entire direction of the plot (it convinces the musician that the girl must be telling the truth).

◀ *Nova Pilbeam in* **Young and Innocent** *(1938). The fugitive is hiding in the loft of an old mill, where the young girl brings him food. Nova Pilbeam previously played the kidnapped daughter in* **The Man Who Knew Too Much** *(1934).*

▶ *Michael Redgrave struggles with the magician (Philip Leaver) in* **The Lady Vanishes** *(1938), while Margaret Lockwood tries to help.*

◀ *Dr Harts (Paul Lukas) and his men fire at the train in* **The Lady Vanishes** *(1938): the Baroness (Mary Clare) watches from the trees. They are trying to prevent the escape of a female spy who is smuggling secrets back to England.*

▶ *Charles Laughton (center) as the wicked judge in* **Jamaica Inn** *(1939), watched by Robert Newton and Maureen O'Hara (left). Laughton is about to climb to the topmast of the ship and then throw himself to his death (death by falling is a common fate in Hitchcock's films). Hitchcock and Laughton did not get on well together, though Laughton's performance remains the most interesting aspect of the film.*

The Lady Vanishes invites comparisons with two other classics of the late 1930s: John Ford's **Stagecoach** (1939) and Jean Renoir's **The Rules of the Game** (1939). Like Ford's film, it is a comic and exciting study of a group of diverse characters on a dangerous journey who reveal their true mettle when tested by an external threat. Like Renoir's film, it offers a picture of a whole society on the eve of world conflict. "England on the brink . . . " is the headline in the newspaper which Charters and Caldicott are reading. It is referring to cricket, but it could also be referring to imminent global conflict in which England will be involved.

"I'm half inclined to believe there's some rational explanation for all this," says Caldicott at one stage. It is a neat, rather provocative comment. Those who take Hitchcock simply on the level of entertainer tend to love **The Lady Vanishes** for its charm, quick wittedness, and comic and narrative invention. Possibilities of political allegory are scarcely acknowledged. The more serious Hitchcock admirer tends to find the film a little superficial, the ingenious mechanisms of plot and technique overriding any complexity of character or response. But it remains one of the best loved of Hitchcock's British films, and for it the New York Film Critics voted him the best director of the year.

Successful failure

Hitchcock was now looking to America. He had been offered a contract by producer David O. Selznick and, after a project on the sinking of the Titanic had been dropped, the opportunity was arising to make a film of Daphne du Maurier's **Rebecca**. There seems little doubt at this time that Hitchcock was ready to leave England. He had always wanted to work in a big Hollywood studio, and it seems clear that he felt he would ultimately become stifled by English insularity and by a snobbish disdain for the cinema in Britain.

Before he left, there was time for one more film, an adaptation of another Daphne du Maurier novel, **Jamaica Inn** (1939), which was a commercial success but an artistic failure. In Hitchcock's words, it was "an absurd thing to undertake". A young Irish girl (Maureen O'Hara), visiting her aunt in Cornwall during the eighteenth century, discovers that Jamaica Inn is the refuge for a gang of cut-throats who lure ships on to the rocks so that they can steal the cargo. She entrusts this knowledge to the local justice of the peace (Charles Laughton), who turns out to be masterminding the whole operation.

The only point of interest in the film is Charles Laughton's performance. This seems out of proportion to the rest but is still an enjoyable study of a divided character, apparently respectable, actually a rogue, an incipient madman who is also capable of kindness and a recognition of beauty. He eventually commits suicide by throwing himself from the mast on to the deck of a ship.

Probably the only thing which drew Hitchcock to the material was a certain identification between himself and the character played by Laughton, a man who feels his obsessive romanticism tragically trapped within a portly, unattractive frame. Otherwise Hitchcock seemed decidedly uneasy with the period setting, and the original yarn's clumsy piratical melodramatics. He wanted a fresh challenge. It was time for the New World.

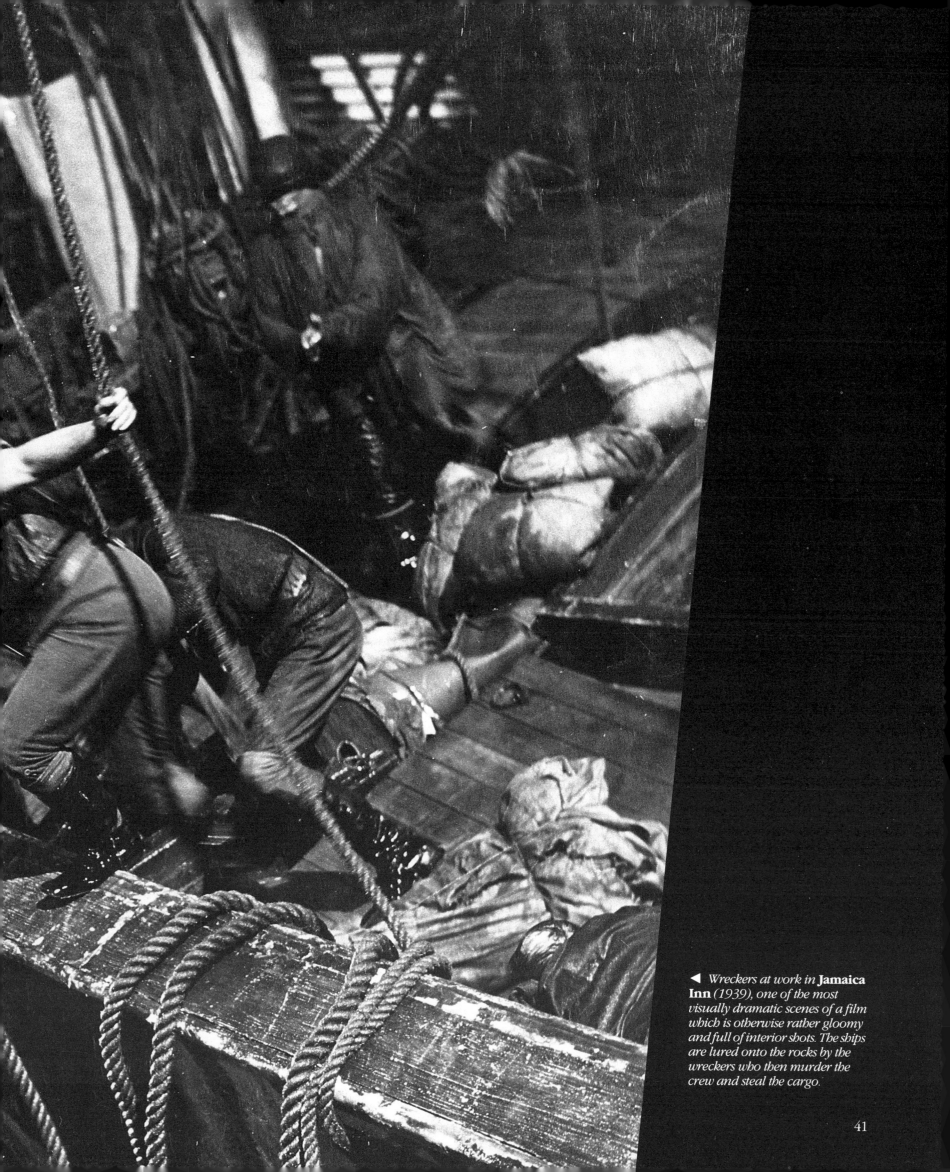

◀ *Wreckers at work in* **Jamaica Inn** *(1939), one of the most visually dramatic scenes of a film which is otherwise rather gloomy and full of interior shots. The ships are lured onto the rocks by the wreckers who then murder the crew and steal the cargo.*

▲ *Ingrid Bergman suspects that her coffee is drugged in* **Notorious** *(1946). Drugged or poisonous drinks, highlighted by the director's careful framing, feature prominently in Hitchcock's films (***The Lady Vanishes***, 1938, and* **Suspicion***, 1941, for example). Bergman was one of Hitchcock's favorite actresses during the decade and brought a new dimension of romanticism into his films.*

itchcock could hardly have begun his career in Hollywood more auspiciously. His first American film, **Rebecca** (1940), won the Best Picture Oscar, the only Hitchcock film ever to do so. In the following year, Joan Fontaine won the Best Actress Oscar for her performance in **Suspicion** (1941), the only Oscar-winning performance in a Hitchcock film, and the director himself was nominated for his work on **Rebecca** and **Lifeboat** (1944).

Some of his early Hollywood films, like **Foreign Correspondent** (1940) and **Saboteur** (1942), do not have strong casts, but gradually Hitchcock's prestige became such that Hollywood's top stars did work for him. It was during this decade that he forged a particularly strong working relationship with Cary Grant and Ingrid Bergman. He also had an especially strong line-up of writers during this period. Lubitsch's brilliant scenarist, Samson Raphaelson, worked on **Suspicion** and the great Ben Hecht wrote **Spellbound** (1945) and **Notorious** (1946). Novelist John Steinbeck wrote the screen story for **Lifeboat**, and the playwright Thornton Wilder made an important contribution to **Shadow of a Doubt** (1943), which Hitchcock appreciated enough to acknowledge his gratitude explicitly on the credits.

Self-imposed challenges

Hitchcock had his fair share of commercial success during the decade. **Suspicion**, **Spellbound** and **Notorious** were three of the most popular thrillers of the 1940s. Even so, in Hitchcock commercial success was not synonymous with caution or conventionality in either style or subject-matter. The innovatory possibilities of film technique still excited him. He shot **Shadow of a Doubt** almost entirely on location, before the post-war demand for realism made this a fashionable thing to do. In both **Lifeboat** and **Rope** (1948) he created suspenseful cinema from the most confined of settings, giving himself a cinematic challenge by selecting material whose chief characteristic was static claustrophobia. **Spellbound** even included a surrealistic dream sequence designed by Salvador Dalí.

Suspense thriller

If technically Hitchcock seemed as daring as ever, thematically the films at first sight continued along the lines laid down in Britain – that is to say, the suspense thriller. His only major deviation from this was a curious screwball comedy, **Mr and Mrs Smith** (1941), written by Norman Krasna and done by Hitchcock as a favor to the film's star, Carole Lombard. In the film her strained marriage to Robert Montgomery is suddenly declared invalid, through a legal

◄ *Carole Lombard and Robert Montgomery in* **Mr and Mrs Smith** *(1941), a screwball comedy about a couple whose strained marriage has been annulled on a technicality but who keep running into each other and eventually get back together again. It was an uncharacteristic venture for Hitchcock, and not successful. "Since I really didn't understand the type of people portrayed in the film," he said, "all I did was to photograph the scenes as written." The writer was Norman Krasna.*

technicality, and the two enjoy a momentary burst of freedom from each other before finding, on a ski-ing holiday, that they really cannot live apart.

The material was in the tradition of classic Hollywood comedies of remarriage, like Leo McCarey's **The Awful Truth** (1937) and George Cukor's **The Philadelphia Story** (1940). Hitchcock attempted to marry the satirical slapstick of a Preston Sturges with the sly and sophisticated sexuality of an Ernst Lubitsch (a shot of crossed skis to imply renewed connubial bliss, for example). There were some deft touches, marital bickerings and embarrassments that recalled Hitchcock's similarly offbeat British film, **Rich and Strange** (1932), and a particularly nice moment of reversal when the man says to the lady: "Excuse me, I'm going to get into something more comfortable." Even so, audiences seemed to miss the frisson of danger and dead bodies; Hitchcock did not care to repeat the experiment.

Hitchcock's Englishness was still evident in his early Hollywood films: **Rebecca** and **Suspicion** were both set in England. Hitchcock's nationality was also suggested by his immediate and undisguised cinematic plea for active support of England against Germany in the Second World War, in contrast to Hollywood's prevalent isolationism at this time.

His anti-Nazi melodrama, **Foreign Correspondent** (1940), has some inventive set-pieces. A political assassin scuttles away from his crime under a crowd of umbrellas; there is a brilliantly shot plane crash, and a clever use of a windmill not only as the setting for sabotage but as a symbol of the Wheel of Fortune in historically turbulent times. Joel McCrea's final speech ("Keep your lights

▲ *Jack Carson looks on as his friend, Robert Montgomery, makes a fool of himself in an elegant Manhattan nightspot in* **Mr and Mrs Smith** *(1941). The two are on a double date and Montgomery is inciting his ex-wife's jealousy. However, the tables are turned when he starts to sneeze and his lady companion forces him to lie back as a cure.*

▶ *The political assassination at Amsterdam Town Hall in the exciting thriller* **Foreign Correspondent** *(1940). The killer poses as a press photographer, shoots his victim with a gun held alongside the camera, and then escapes under a sea of umbrellas.* **Foreign Correspondent** *is an overtly anti-Nazi tract, quite outspoken at a period of American neutrality and considered by Goebbels as a "remarkable and very dangerous film".*

◀ *Joel McCrea hides from his pursuers in a windmill in* **Foreign Correspondent** *(1940). The windmill is being used by the Nazis to signal to approaching airplanes. This shot is a good example of Hitchcock's dictum that part of a film-maker's responsibility was not simply to choose a location but to use it. The windmill provides local color, is a wide-ranging dramatic symbol and an invaluable part of the plot.*

▼ *Robert Cummings makes his getaway in* **Saboteur** *(1942) by hiding under a bridge. Cummings plays a factory worker framed for arson, who is equally anxious to avoid capture and find the criminals. Hitchcock particularly liked the double-hunt structure, perhaps most famously developed in* **The 39 Steps** *(1935) and* **North by Northwest** *(1959).*

burning, America"), written by Ben Hecht, was a powerful piece of propaganda designed to influence America in abandoning its neutral foreign policy and joining England and Europe in the fight against Fascism.

Saboteur (1942) seemed an American farewell to Hitchcock's English period of the 1930s. As in **The 39 Steps**, there is an innocent handcuffed man on the run. As in **Sabotage**, action on a cinema screen counterpoints the action that is taking place in the auditorium. Robert Cummings plays the pursued man who uncovers a nest of American Nazis. An encounter with circus freaks is sensitively done, but again, as in **Foreign Correspondent**, the thing which distinguishes the film from its English predecessors is the urgency of its imagery. The Nazi saboteur, for example, finally plunges to his death from the Statue of Liberty, a symbolic ending clearly designed to assert the ultimate victory of freedom over Fascism. In 1944, Hitchcock also made a couple of short French-language propaganda films in England for the Ministry of Information, **Bon Voyage** and **Aventure Malgache**, thrillers intended as tributes to the French Resistance.

▲ Robert Cummings and
Priscilla Lane in a scene from
Saboteur (1942). Although he
tries to convince her that he is
innocent, she is more persuaded
by the handcuffs. Like Donat in
The 39 Steps (1935), Cummings
spends much of the film in
handcuffs. They crop up
emphatically in other Hitchcock
movies – **The Lodger** (1926-27)
and **The Wrong Man** (1956).
"Being tied to something ..."
Hitchcock said innocently, "it's
somewhere in the area of
fetishism, isn't it?"

Controversial contribution

Hitchcock's most controversial cinematic contribution to the war effort was in **Lifeboat** (1944). A group of survivors from a torpedoed freighter are joined on their lifeboat by a German who was on the attacking U-boat, which has also sunk. They need his navigational expertise to survive but when they discover that he has been guiding their lifeboat towards a German supply ship, they beat him to death.

The controversy stemmed from a certain ambiguity in characterization and theme. Hitchcock intended it as an allegory showing the necessity for believers in democracy (the cross-section of humanity on the lifeboat) to sink their differences in the common goal of defeating Fascism. However, some critics objected to the way the Nazi seems smarter than all the democrats put together, the ugly brutality of his murder, and the fact that the message by that time seemed a little late.

The ambiguity is compounded by the uneven performances. Walter Slezak creates a complex, intelligent characterization out of the Nazi. Tallulah Bankhead is outstanding as the socialite who sheds her prejudices and her trinkets for the common good. But the remainder of the cast are rather two-dimensional. Hitchcock rises to the challenge of sustaining visual interest in a confined setting, and, although the material is basically intended to further a cause, it gives a hint of the increasing moral complexity of his work.

▼ *Hume Cronyn, William Bendix and Heather Angel in* **Lifeboat** *(1944). Most of the film was shot in the studio tank at Twentieth Century-Fox. The film was undertaken by Hitchcock "because I wanted to prove a theory I had then. Analyzing the psychological pictures that were being turned out, it seemed to me that, visually, 80 percent of the footage was shot in close-ups or semi-close shots. Most likely it wasn't a conscious thing with most directors but rather an instinctive need to come closer to the action."*

Lifeboat (1944).

◄ *A desperate moment for the lifeboat crew. From left to right: John Hodiak, Tallulah Bankhead, William Bendix, Henry Hull, Mary Anderson and, with his back turned, Walter Slezak.*

▼ *Henry Hull converses with Tallulah Bankhead. She was voted Actress of the Year by the New York film critics for her performance as a society journalist.*

Adoration and sadism

It was not surprising that, like other European emigré filmmakers who had settled in Hollywood, Hitchcock's film-making during the war period was more propagandist and controversial than before. More significant was the appearance of several new dimensions in his films that had not been evident in his British work and indeed which might have been suppressed if he had remained in England. Somehow the cultural cosmopolitanism of America and the more expansive resources of Hollywood released hitherto unsuspected facets in Hitchcock's film-making and personality.

Three elements particularly come increasingly to the fore: his complex, lurking and often lurid romanticism; his treatment of women in his films, which lurches disturbingly between adoration and sadism; and an unexpected and increasing darkness of tone, a grimness of theme and impact that is sometimes unalleviated by comedy.

The romantic Hitchcock is well exemplified by **Rebecca**, the first of four films he made under the aegis of David Selznick. Selznick's own romanticism undoubtedly contributed much to the final effect. Nevertheless, for all Selznick's influence and his insistence that Hitchcock adhere as faithfully as possible to the outline of Daphne du Maurier's classic novel, the personality of the director does come through quite strongly, and it is not the personality one might have expected from his previous films. Part of the reason why **Rebecca** has maintained its fascination is that it looks ahead to subsequent major Hitchcock films, notably **Vertigo** (1958).

Offbeat visual details

The convention is to see **Rebecca** as essentially a faithful adaptation of the novel, garnished with a few Hitchcock touches. The story is still that of a timid companion (Joan Fontaine) who is swept off her feet by the dashing Maxim De Winter (Laurence Olivier). She becomes caught up in the mystery of the house, Manderley; of what happened to Maxim's first wife, Rebecca; and of what motivates the sinister housekeeper, Mrs Danvers (Judith Anderson).

Hitchcock elaborates this basic outline with typically offbeat visual details. Early in the film the heroine's employer, Mrs Van Hopper, stubs out her cigarette in a jar of cleansing cream, an anticipation of a more famous Hitchcock image in **To Catch a Thief** (1955), when Jessie Royce Landis disposes of her cigarette end in the yolk of a fried egg. Mrs Danvers is made particularly sinister by the strict, dehumanized choreography of her almost inaudible movements. As the heroine's jealousy of the spirit of Rebecca begins to grow, Hitchcock includes a splendidly shot scene where pictures from a home movie of their idyllic honeymoon counterpoint the de Winters' marital bickering and the calculated cruelty of Maxim's comment to his young wife: "Happiness is something I know very little about."

▶ *The young heroine (Joan Fontaine, center) in* **Rebecca** *(1940) pretends to her employer (Florence Bates, right) that she is about to have a tennis lesson so that she can secretly meet the mysterious Maxim de Winter.*

Recurring themes

However, **Rebecca** has a more central place in Hitchcock's work than this general description would imply. For example, the approach to Manderley at the beginning is filmed in a manner similar to the approach to the motel in **Psycho** – the building is glimpsed through a windscreen wiper shot in the rain. As in **Psycho** (1960), the house is felt as a person, filled with the spirit of someone long dead, but whose presence is sensed through objects like napkins, stationery, pillowcases, and a dress.

The relationship between the heroine and Mrs Danvers – victim and tormentor, rabbit hypnotized by a snake – is one that will be repeated in future Hitchcock encounters, like that of heroine and housekeeper in **Under Capricorn** (1949), tennis star and psychopath in **Strangers on a Train** (1951), or thief and traffic cop in **Psycho**.

As in **Vertigo**, we are introduced to the hero hovering over a precipice (something not in the original novel). Both films have the

Rebecca (1940).
◀ Mrs Danvers (Judith Anderson, right) tempts the heroine (Joan Fontaine) into thoughts of suicide. This is a characteristic Hitchcock image of victim and tormentor framed together. Hitchcock's couples are often really triangles, but with a missing third party (for example the scenes between Cary Grant and Ingrid Bergman in **Notorious**, 1946, or James Stewart and Kim Novak in the last third of **Vertigo**, 1958). In this scene from **Rebecca**, the missing third party is the spirit of Rebecca herself, still idolized by Mrs Danvers and still tormenting the hapless heroine.

▼ A villager testifies at the inquest watched tensely by Maxim (Laurence Olivier, seated in background, second left). The small room and low roof add to the atmosphere of claustrophobia and oppression.

same obsession of the hero for a dead woman, and include his traumatic confrontation with her 'proxy' midway through the action. In **Rebecca**, this occurs when his wife appears to Maxim in a copy of the dress worn, unknown to her, by Rebecca at a previous fancy-dress ball. Maxim's reaction of shock and disgust is rather like the hero's reaction in **Vertigo** to his girlfriend's parody portrait of the woman who has become the object of his desire. In both films, the ocean is used to punctuate moments of turbulent emotion, and there is a similarly edgy and unsettling scene at an inquest.

Rebecca is nowhere near as fine an achievement as the later film, being melodramatic where the latter is poetic, and becoming increasingly bogged down in plot after the shock revelation that Maxim hated Rebecca and is indirectly responsible for her death. On the whole, though, **Rebecca** is an unexpected glimpse of a side to Hitchcock barely suspected in England but which emerged with enormous potency in his American films: Hitchcock the tortured Romantic.

S.I.P-110-71

Laurence Olivier as the dashing Maxim, Judith Anderson as the chilling Mrs Danvers, and George Sanders as a suave blackmailer give predictably fine performances. The surprise is Joan Fontaine, who was preferred over Margaret Sullavan and Anne Baxter for the main role of the young Heroine With No Name (Hitchcock characteristically wanted to call her "Daphne" but Selznick insisted they be faithful to the novel and leave her nameless).

Much of the film's suspense comes not from obvious thriller events and tactics but from the heroine's social gaucheness, her embarrassment, and her tiny moments of clumsy indiscretion (like her breaking of an ornament) that grow into crises through her frightened but futile attempts at concealment. Joan Fontaine's performance might be so good because she was, by her own account, terrified by the whole experience and particularly by Hitchcock and Olivier who completely overawed her.

Desire to destroy

Hitchcock's sensitivity to the tremors of female feeling in **Rebecca** is counterbalanced, one feels, by a mischievous and almost malicious delight in contriving another ingenious incident of embarrassment and humiliation for her. Hitchcock's heroines are adored, but they suffer for that adoration, and Hitchcock's yearning admiration of them seems perversely mingled with a desire to violate and destroy. The punishment undergone by the heroines in, for example, **Notorious**, **Under Capricorn**, **Dial M for Murder** (1954), **The Birds** (1963) and **Marnie** (1964) seems out of all proportion to their vices of passivity or deceit.

We begin to notice the peculiar combination of fear and desire in the sexual relationships in Hitchcock's films. The women, in particular, have to adjust to men who are at times protective and at other times predatory, and whose devotion might at any time slip to a hatred of women that could be murderous. A good example of that is **Suspicion**, made a year after **Rebecca**.

Joan Fontaine plays a shy society girl who falls for a wastrel, Johnny Aysgarth (Cary Grant), first encountered when she hears his disembodied voice talking to her as their train goes through a tunnel. (An accidental meeting on a train is to provide similarly sinister developments in **Strangers on a Train**. The saucy sexual symbolism of train entering a tunnel is to be explicitly deployed in the Freudian final shot of **North by Northwest**, 1959.) They marry, but she begins to discover evidence of deceit and duplicity and suspect he has married her for her money. As his money problems intensify, she slowly realizes that he is planning to kill her.

Murderous ambiguity

Suspicion is one of Hitchcock's most ambiguous films, and its suspense comes from a variety of sources. One of the reasons why the heroine is disposed to believe the worst about her husband stems from her own lack of self-confidence: why would a handsome man like him be interested in a dull creature like herself if it were not for her money? Also, there is some doubt about the justification of her suspicions. In a word game one evening, she almost subconsciously spells out the word 'Murder' and seems to foresee the death of Johnny's friend and business partner, Beaky (Nigel Bruce); but is this an over-active imagination?

Her suspicions begin increasingly to reveal as much about her as about her husband: her sheltered and repressed upbringing, and, as a corollary of that, the sense in which she almost wills herself into believing her husband is a murderer (in the way that the hero almost wills the murder in **Rear Window**) to animate and bring excitement into her stultified existence.

In Francis Iles's original novel, entitled *Before the Fact* because the wife is an accomplice in her own death, the husband is revealed as a murderer. Hitchcock expressed some dissatisfaction that he was not allowed to repeat this in the film because, so he said, audiences would not accept Cary Grant as a killer. The admission has been seized on by Hitchcock detractors as a typical example of Hitchcockian compromise. However, as the film stands, the sustained ambiguity is, if anything, more aesthetically satisfying and provides more tension.

The film becomes a study of the ambiguity of circumstantial evidence and visual appearance, and of how to arouse an audience's sense of suspicion to such a pitch that, at one moment, the most sinister thing in the world can seem a bedtime glass of milk. In the final scene, it is quite impossible to tell from the visual evidence whether the husband is trying to push his wife out of the car to her death, or, as he claims, trying to prevent her from jumping as suspicion has now pushed her to the edge of hysteria.

His final explanation of his behavior is no more nor less convincing than any of the others, and the ostensibly happy ending, when he turns the car to drive back home, is modified by his gesture of stretching his arm around the back of her neck. Is this a gesture of endearment or confidence, a recognition that she might be more vulnerable now that her guard has been lowered? Joan Fontaine deservedly won an Oscar, and the desperation and Dionysiac darkness that lurks beneath Cary Grant's easy playboy charm have rarely been more powerfully exploited. Until **Notorious**, that is.

Victim of neurosis

Curiously, Hitchcock's second film for David Selznick, **Spellbound** (1945), has a similar situation to **Suspicion**, crudely but accurately set out in the film's advertising slogan: "Will he kiss me, or kill me?" Ingrid Bergman's analyst falls for a doctor (Gregory Peck) who turns out to be an impostor and suspected murderer. He also has recurrent nightmares involving straight lines and the color white, which may hold the clue to his past and identity.

The woman's courageous, almost sacrificial attempt to release the hero from his trauma involves placing herself in situations of extreme peril, making her the prey and possible victim of the man's neurosis and violent fantasies. Unlike **Notorious** and **Marnie**, however, where the heroines endure purgatory because of the sexual hang-ups of their men, **Spellbound** ends harmoniously. In truth, it is one of Hitchcock's most gimmicky pictures, with Dalí's interpolated fantasy sequence being disappointingly literal (a wheel turns out to mean "revolver", for example), and with the suicide of the guilty party being shown by a giant hand turning a gun towards the camera and a red flash suffusing the screen as the trigger is pulled.

▶ *Cary Grant is the sinister figure on the stairs, taking his wife a nightcap in* **Suspicion** *(1941), which could just be her last. "I put a light right inside the glass because I wanted it to be luminous," said Hitch. "Cary Grant is walking up the stairs so everyone's attention had to be focused on that glass."*

Suspicion *(1941).*

▼ *The final scene. Joan Fontaine is now convinced that her husband wants to kill her but, in trying to escape from the car, seems likely to end up killing herself. The critics Rohmer and Chabrol said that: "She feeds on her suspicion like a vampire. She wants to wallow in the failure of her love."*

▶ *A similar design to this poster was later used to advertise* **Spellbound** *(1945).*

▶ *While Ingrid Bergman sleeps in* **Spellbound** *(1945), Gregory Peck enacts the fear that roams her subconscious: the fear that the man she loves may be a murderer. Peck has been terrified by the glaring white color of a bathroom and lines on a bathrobe that trigger a buried childhood trauma. The critic James Agee commented: "In one crisis of mental dereliction in which the camera flicks its eye forlornly round a bathroom, you get a little of the unlimited, cryptic terror that can reside in mere objects."*

Curiously, the red flash and the Freudian themes of the film are to recur in the later and much more profound work, **Marnie**. But **Spellbound** does usefully illustrate the way Hitchcock was going more and more into Freudian themes and tortured sexual relationships as the basis of suspense, and into the proximity between film and dream. "Good night and sweet dreams," says Ingrid Bergman's psychology professor (a fine performance by Michael Chekhov), before adding: "which we will analyze at breakfast." Hitchcock's films will increasingly become the dreams in the dark of a very complicated man.

Spellbound (1945).
◀ Ingrid Bergman bravely embraces Gregory Peck and the danger which he represents.

▶ A detail from the dream sequence designed by Salvador Dalí. "I wanted Dalí because of the architectural sharpness of his work," said Hitch. "Chirico has the same quality, the long shadows, the infinity of distance, and the converging lines of perspective." According to Ingrid Bergman, the original dream lasted 20 minutes and was a surrealist masterpiece in its own right.

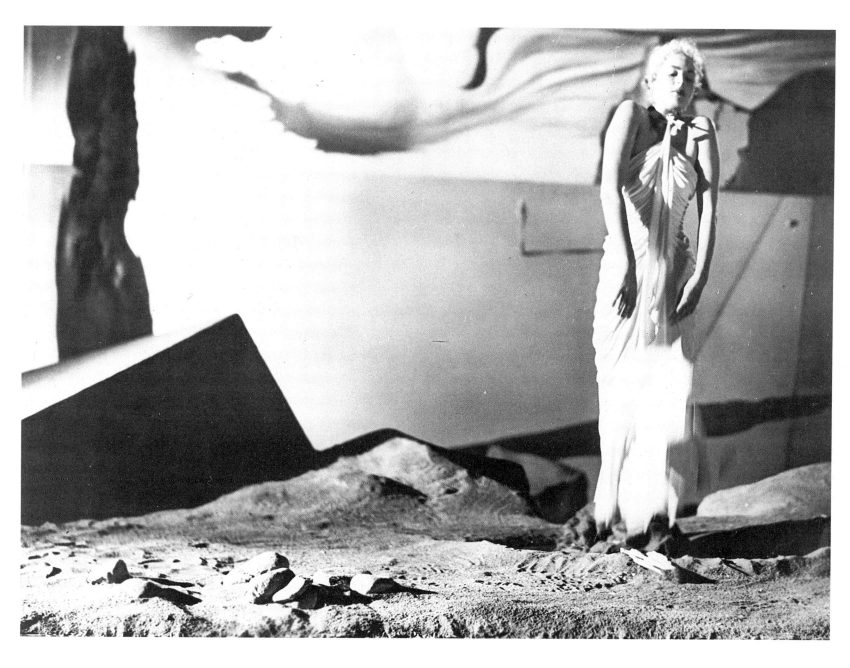

Dark masterpieces

Were Hitchcock's films of the 1940s growing more serious, or just slower? Hollywood, or something, seemed to have wiped the smile off his face. The decade did not produce a single film that could really be called a comedy thriller, and, for some Hitchcock aficionados, the films were beginning to seem as bulky as the portly frame of their director. They missed the sparkle and sprightliness of the English period. To them, America seemed to have turned Hitchcock into a more dour and lugubrious fellow.

However, it is possible to equate this so-called sparkle with superficiality, and see the dourness as a conscious and fascinating darkening of tone, the increasingly profound expression of a personal misanthropy, anguish and romantic obsession. **Shadow of a Doubt** (1943) and **Notorious** are the quintessential examples of this more serious Hitchcock. They also seem to me Hitchcock's two undoubted masterpieces of the decade.

The central character of **Shadow of a Doubt** is Uncle Charlie (Joseph Cotten), who comes to visit his relatives in Santa Rosa, California. His niece, also called Charlie (Teresa Wright), idolizes him. However, her hero-worship turns to suspicion that he is a murderer on the run when two policemen posing as pollsters turn up on her doorstep with inquiries about him. Ironically, their suspicions of Uncle Charlie are allayed at the moment when hers are confirmed, and the finale of the film is a life-and-death struggle between the two Charlies whose love for each other has now turned to hate.

Several things contribute to the remarkable and enduring success of the film. The location shooting seems to have had a bracing effect on Hitchcock. The film has an air, conviction and realism that is quite opposed to the atmosphere of studio-stale melodrama that sometimes clung to his earlier pictures. The authenticity is enhanced by genuinely three-dimensional characterization and, for the first time in Hitchcock, the suspense is generated more through character complexity than situational contrivance.

Because of the finely written roles, the film also emerges as, and remains, the best acted of any of Hitchcock's movies. Joseph Cotten and Teresa Wright bring out the poignancy and pain of the uncle/niece relationship with rare sensitivity, and the supporting performances of young Charlie's ponderous father (Henry Travers), her bookish younger sister (Edna May Wonacott gives the best child performance in a Hitchcock film) and her timid neighbor (Hume Cronyn) are equally fine. Perhaps most moving of all is Patricia Col-

Shadow of a Doubt (1943). The film is about a loving relationship between uncle and niece that turns to tension and hatred when the girl begins to suspect that Uncle Charlie is the "Merry Widow" murderer being hunted across the country.
◄ Joseph Cotten's gesture towards Teresa Wright seems simultaneously affectionate and murderous.

▲ Hitchcock on location in Santa Rosa preparing to shoot the scene of Uncle Charlie's arrival. Next to Hitchcock are Teresa Wright, Edna May Wonacott as her studious sister, Charlie Bates as her young brother and Henry Travers as her father. In researching the film, Hitchcock and his writer, Thornton Wilder, stayed in Santa Rosa to get to know the character and nature of the town and its people.

▲ *Almost suffocated by carbon monoxide fumes, Teresa Wright pushes open the door of the garage. This is her uncle's second attempt to murder her.*

linge as young Charlie's mother and Uncle Charlie's sister, the most sympathetic maternal characterization in Hitchcock. Heart-rending in her farewell to her brother, she flaps around the kitchen with a domestic fussiness that implies volumes about an unsatisfied repressed vitality that has been unable to find an outlet.

The film could be read as an allegory of good and evil, the innocent heroine fascinated by, yet at the end forcibly fending off, the influence of an outwardly debonair, inwardly demonic character. However, it is more complicated than that. The two characters are closely wedded together: indeed, Charlie does give his niece a ring at one point. They are both visually introduced in the same pose, lying on a bed, and young Charlie says at one stage that they are "sort of like twins", almost mirror reflections of a single personality.

Uncle Charlie is not evil incarnate, any more than young Charlie is the personification of good. She might be said to symbolize her uncle's good side, his charm, his love of his family, and perhaps also the moral righteousness that has driven him to kill. He is young Charlie's shadow side, the fulfillment of her craving for excitement, the embodiment of the knowledge of the darker side of the world that she must acquire in order to achieve maturity.

Double theme

Shadow of a Doubt is the first thorough treatment in Hitchcock of a theme which will recur increasingly in his work: that of the Double. It recurs in several different guises (the pursuit of the wrong man, the theme of mistaken identity), but it often takes the form of a "good" character being made aware, through confrontation with another, of a darker side to the world and his own character hitherto unsuspected. (**Strangers on a Train** is the most obvious other example.)

Everything in **Shadow of a Doubt** seems to move in pairs: two Charlies, two policemen, two scenes in a garage, two at the dinner table and so on. Is the family's cosiness charming or, as the daughter finds it, oppressive? Is Uncle Charlie a Devil or a kind of tragic hero, striking out at the materialism and sterility of the modern world?

At the end, after Uncle Charlie's death (he has fallen under a train after attempting to kill his niece), the town pays tribute to him as a hero and benefactor. Beneath the surface of the service, as it were, the niece tells the truth about him to the young policeman (MacDonald Carey). Normality has been restored but only at the cost of suppressing the truth, a truth which seems to expose the desolation of conventional bourgeois life.

The implication is that young Charlie will marry the policeman and hence perpetuate a family life that has been revealed as spiritually impoverished. There is a feeling also that the man she truly loved has perished under that train. In interviews, often in unlikely contexts, Hitchcock was prone to quote Oscar Wilde's "Each man kills the thing he loves." Love and hate are closely akin emotions in Hitchcock's films and **Shadow of a Doubt** is not the only one in which a character, either inadvertently or deliberately, causes the death of the person he or she loves.

Freudian discontent

The theme of **Shadow of a Doubt** is basically Freudian: the discontents of civilization. The urgency of its theme perhaps comes from the period in which it was made. Its theme of the spread of evil, awakening people from their complacency, could be seen as a warning to America after Pearl Harbor. The recurrent image of couples dancing to Franz Lehár's "Merry Widow Waltz" seems not only an image of elegance that represents the idealized past of which Uncle Charlie talks: its hysterical edge (in Dimitri Tiomkin's snarling orchestration) takes the feeling closer to the neurosis of Ravel's "La Valse", which aurally conveys the collapse of a civilized world into a new barbarity.

Hitchcock's direction is a model of economy and precision. There are no flashy set-pieces, but a careful marshaling of images and symbols (the ring, the menacing black smoke that billows out of the train to herald Uncle Charlie's arrival, his brandished cigar as image of control and confidence) to underline the themes and augment the performances. It is not only one of the first and best examples of Hollywood *film noir*, bringing to light the shadow side of human personality. It is the first modern American horror film, not only glimpsing the world as "a foul sty" but rooting the sources of horror, frustration and violence in the heart of average family life.

Menacing symbols

Hitchcock's second outstanding film of the decade, **Notorious** (1946), brilliantly scripted by Ben Hecht, is perhaps less resonant

about modern life and less moving about personal relationships than **Shadow of a Doubt**. It is still one of Hitchcock's most intense studies of tormented love. Ingrid Bergman plays Alicia, the daughter of a Nazi who has just been convicted of espionage. Knowing that Alicia opposed the ideas of her father but will nevertheless be able to exploit his connections, the FBI recruit her to infiltrate an underground Fascist organization, headed by Alex Sebastian (Claude Rains). The situation is complicated when she falls in love with her FBI contact, Devlin (Cary Grant), and Sebastian proposes marriage to her.

As a spy thriller, **Notorious** accomplishes an enormous amount with a minimum of means. The plot almost entirely abstains from violence. Instead, it proceeds with a stealthy, implacable logic in which simple objects like a key or a bottle of champagne suddenly become charged with drama and menace.

The use of drink in the film is a means of carrying important narrative and thematic points. It first of all establishes the heroine's potential for alcoholism. Devlin's disquiet when he learns of the FBI plot to loose Alicia on Sebastian is symbolized by an unopened bottle of champagne, which he has planned to take to Alicia and which, in his agitation, he leaves at the FBI office. The secret of the underground organization's new bomb is hidden in a wine bottle. The film's suspense set-piece is the wine cellar search by Devlin and Alicia for this secret during one of Sebastian's parties, a scene introduced by an astonishing continuous camera movement which begins with an overhead view of the whole party and ends on a close-up of the cellar key clasped in the heroine's hand. Finally, when Sebastian learns of Alicia's betrayal, the most important object becomes a poisoned cup of coffee which is persistently proffered to Alicia. Will Devlin correctly interpret Alicia's decline in their secret meetings, or will he simply think that she is at the bottle again? Is he so poisoned by jealousy, bitterness and cynicism that he will overlook the truth?

In fact, it is poisoned love more than poisoned drinks that provides the substance of the film. Politically, **Notorious** is remarkably evenhanded: the American agents are scarcely more sympathetic than their enemies and, in some ways, less so. (One cannot forget the detail of the Americans sending Alicia to seduce Sebastian with *rented* jewelry.)

The espionage theme seems more a vehicle to explore the themes of trust and betrayal, devotion and deception in human relationships, and particularly to explore the vicissitudes of love. Parental love is seen to be contaminated, first of all: Alicia had a love/hate relationship with her Nazi father, who finally poisoned himself in his prison cell. Sebastian is in thrall to his dominating mother (Leopoldine Konstantin), whose instant distrust of Alicia has as much to do with jealousy as political perception. Most extraordinary, though, is the central love triangle between Alicia, who experiences love as torture, Devlin, who feels it as pain, and Sebastian, who describes it as hunger. The relationship between Alicia and Devlin recounts a painful struggle of two bruised personalities to break through past disillusionments into a mature commitment.

Cary Grant's unsmiling performance as Devlin is bloodchilling: the actor's supreme gift for comedy is here simply used to give the cynical and spiteful nuances of his dialogue an extra twist of the knife. Part of the tension in the film comes from the fact that he seems to care less about the heroine than does Sebastian, played with aching sincerity by Claude Rains in a performance that was

Notorious (1946).
▼ Ingrid Bergman collapses at the foot of the stairs. She is convinced that her husband and his mother are trying to kill her but is powerless to prevent them.

▶ Cary Grant to the rescue. For the first time in the film he honestly expresses his love. Grant, unsmiling throughout, gives one of his most compelling dramatic performances: Ingrid Bergman is equally fine.

deservedly nominated for an Oscar. In the center is Ingrid Bergman, as a heroine who suffers abuse emotionally, sexually and politically.

Behind the suspenseful insinuations of Hitchcock's camera in **Notorious** lurks a remarkably bold study of political cold-bloodedness and emotional hypocrisy. The suspense lies in the desolation of thwarted love relationships and in whether the central characters can break through their failures of communication.

Marking time

It was to be some time before Hitchcock managed to duplicate the artistic and commercial success of **Notorious**. His next four films are among the most problematical of his career, all having their interesting moments but offering no clear indication of where Hitchcock thought he was going. Courtroom drama, technical experiment and two films in England – for the moment, Hitchcock seemed to be marking time.

The Paradine Case (1947) was the last of Hitchcock's films for producer David Selznick, who also wrote the screenplay. It shares some of the themes of **Notorious** – degradation, the conflict between professional objectivity and personal involvement – but on a much lower heat. A defense lawyer (Gregory Peck) falls in love

The Paradine Case (1947).
▼ *Alida Valli (center) plays a woman charged with murdering her husband. Charles Coburn (2nd right) is her lawyer. Hitchcock was interested in a character from a privileged background having to submit to police formalities, and gradually being stripped of freedom and identity. "It may be an expression of my own fear," he said, "but I've always felt the drama of a situation in which a normal person is suddenly deprived of freedom and incarcerated with hardened criminals."*

▶ *Defense counsel Gregory Peck (left) sternly cross-examines the groom (Louis Jourdan), whose secret lover is the defendant in the dock (Alida Valli).*

with his client, Mrs Paradine (Alida Valli), who is accused of murdering her blind husband. The lawyer discovers that Mrs Paradine has had an affair with her groom (Louis Jourdan), and his cross-examination of the groom in the witness box, attempting to implicate him in the murder, precipitates the groom's suicide. A bigger shock is to come. In her grief at her lover's death, Mrs Paradine reveals in court that her lawyer has been blinded by his infatuation for her and that she is guilty of the crime of which she is accused.

It is all rather somber and slow. Gregory Peck is not an actor who can easily convey romantic obsession, and Hitchcock's camera and Franz Waxman's music often have to supply it for him. The trial scenes are reasonably gripping, and one aerial shot of the defense lawyer, leaving the court after the shock disclosure, conveys a crushing sense of isolation and humiliation.

The opening is crisp and concise, as the arrival of the police brings chaos into Mrs Paradine's previously ordered life. Otherwise it is rather predictable, and the casting, in addition to Peck, is not ideal: Alida Valli is too remote to be a vehicle for obsession; Ann Todd, as the lawyer's wife, too cold to evoke sympathy; Louis Jourdan too suave to convey the groom's raw sexual attraction. Charles Laughton, as a sadistic judge with a sensual yen for the lawyer's wife, has by far the best role and gives the juiciest performance.

Hitchcock's technical "stunt"

Technical innovation was to be the main attraction of Hitchcock's next film, **Rope** (1948). It is based on a Patrick Hamilton play about two brilliant young men, Brandon (John Dall) and Philip (Farley Granger), who commit a murder for the hell of it. They then throw a dinner party for the victim's relations and friends, the body being hidden in a trunk on which the dinner is served. One of the guests, their college professor Rupert (James Stewart), whose lectures on the Nietzschean "Superman" concept gave them the idea in the first place, slowly begins to sense what has happened and finally confronts the young men.

Rope was Hitchcock's first film in color, but a much more radical technical challenge was also involved. Because the action takes place roughly between 7.30 and 9 p.m. Hitchcock tried to preserve the unity of time and place with a corresponding unity of camera movement. Rather than cutting up the action by the usual montage and different camera set-ups, he filmed **Rope** in eight ten-minute takes (ten minutes being approximately the amount of film in the camera magazine before it runs out).

Hitchcock afterwards was to refer to the device as "a stunt". Certainly, except in the last case (when Rupert lifts the lid of the trunk and the screen goes black as his worst fears are confirmed), the transitions from one take to the next are both perceptible and awkward.

"Why *not* cut?" asked fellow film-maker Billy Wilder incredulously, clearly thinking Hitchcock was needlessly making problems for himself. "This is writing the Lord's Prayer on the head of a pin. What is he trying to prove?"

James Stewart simply felt that the obtrusive ingenuity of the technique made the slightness of the material all the more obvious. "You're really missing out on a wonderful opportunity here," he told Hitchcock. "You ought to charge people five bucks to come in and see the set rather than the movie, because the movement of the camera and the walls and everything is much more interesting than what we're saying."

Given that the film is basically a technical exercise, it is generally a stimulating one. The ten-minute take not only preserves unity and coherence but emphasizes a sense of claustrophobia as the action and camera movement narrow from three rooms, to two, then one. The camera roams like an inquisitive and uninvited guest. Sometimes it follows the characters. At one stage it becomes hypnotized by a maid who, unnoticed by everyone, is clearing the dinner things and preparing to replace the books in the trunk. At another the camera takes up a position that produces a composition at the heart of the film's meaning. It is the moment when the inspirer of the murder, Rupert, steps in front of its instigator, Brandon, who is in front of its perpetrator, Philip, and we suddenly have a complete chain of responsibility.

If **Rope** is technique without heart, this is formally quite appropriate for a work about a murder committed as a technical exercise. The two young men think of their murder basically as a

Rope (1948).

▲ *James Stewart (center) is about to open the trunk in which his worst fears will be confirmed. Farley Granger (left) looks apprehensive; John Dall (right) defiant. Notice the books on the trunk and Stewart placed center frame, suggesting that his teaching and bookish theorizing have led to the murder.*

▶ *Hitchcock lines up a ten-minute take for his first color film. James Stewart (center) is beginning to find something suspicious in the behavior of his two student hosts, Farley Granger and John Dall (right).*

work of art. Hitchcock is the director who, above all others, has made an art form from the subject of murder. His films are rather like the action of **Rope** – an exhilaratingly uncomfortable party to which we come because we suspect a body might be hidden.

Like Hitchcock, James Stewart's professor is fascinated by the subject of murder but appalled by the action. Like Hitchcock, the professor, with some personal disquiet, reveals himself as a traditional moralist after all. He fires the gun into the street to alert the police and then sits apart from the two young men awaiting the law's arrival – his posture not that of an accomplice, but a judge.

Rupert has talked lightly, theoretically about murder, like young Charlie's father and his friend in **Shadow of a Doubt** or the old ladies at the dinner party in **Strangers on a Train**. The reality of murder will strike back at them, threatening both their lives and their true values.

Although as much about the potentialities of the film camera as the meaning of life, **Rope** does expose the intellectual arrogance of a man whose cynical contempt for humanity has been taken to nightmarish extremes by his young disciples. Indeed, the professor's theoretical justification of murder as a demonstration of superiority over one's conventional and timid fellows might have carried uncomfortable shock waves for an audience recovering from a war generated by a murderous megalomaniac with a similar arrogance and contempt for humanity. Brandon and Philip have the chilling arrogance of the Hitler Youth. **Rope** finally might have as much to say about Fascism as film fashion.

Eccentric project

Hitchcock followed his most bizarre technical experiment with one of his most bizarre subjects, **Under Capricorn** (1949). He returned to England to make it, and it also represents a return to costume melodrama, the previous example (**Jamaica Inn**) prefacing Hitchcock's departure from England to America in the first place.

"I hate costume pictures," he said later, "and haven't bothered to appear in the couple I've made. I was once asked at the San Francisco press club why I didn't make costume pictures, and I said: 'One, I'm not good at it and two, for me, nobody in a costume picture ever goes to the toilet!'"

The attraction of **Under Capricorn** basically seems to have been the opportunity to work again with Ingrid Bergman and to show off his star actress in his former surroundings. Nevertheless, the very eccentricity of the project gives it an unusual fascination.

The story is set in Australia in the 1830s. The Governor-General's Irish nephew, Adare (Michael Wilding), is befriended by an Australian businessman, Flusky (Joseph Cotten), and Flusky's wife (Ingrid Bergman) whom he had known formerly in Ireland. Flusky was a former convict sent from Ireland to Australia for killing his wife's brother. She was a noble lady and Flusky her groom, whose marriage scandalized the country. She had followed Flusky to Australia, but is now an alcoholic. In trying to rehabilitate her, the Irishman discovers that it was she who killed her brother and that Flusky took the blame on her behalf.

For a while, with its faltering accents, period trappings, talky screenplay and stately tempo, **Under Capricorn** does not seem like a Hitchcock movie at all. Suddenly it becomes a movie that could not possibly have been made by anyone else.

The first moment of pure Hitchcock is Adare's visit to the Flusky house. No one films apprehensive approaches to strange places with quite the same tension as Hitchcock. (Think of the sister's approach to the mysterious Bates' house in **Psycho**.) What follows is another remarkable ten-minute take, enclosing the Irishman's approach, his observation of the household, the introduction of the other guests, and stopping only on Flusky's tense expression when he realizes that his wife has unexpectedly entered the dining room behind the Irishman. The other ten-minute take encompasses the wife's confession of her part in her brother's death, the take seeming to emphasize the disclosure as a single unstoppable exhalation of exorcized guilt. It is Ingrid Bergman's finest piece of acting for Hitchcock or, indeed, for anyone.

Characteristic motifs

Under Capricorn might initially seem simply a monument to Hitchcock's favorite leading actress of the time, but gradually more characteristic motifs emerge. It is a film about the pain of love, and about a tortured relationship in which each partner has alternately taken on the mantle of guilt or punishment, suffering or sacrifice, confession or conviction. Even the housekeeper Milly (superbly played by Margaret Leighton) is driven almost to kill because of her love for Flusky and her consequent determination to demoralize and destroy his wife. Adare is also drawn into the pain of sacrifice. His testimony regarding his wound saves Flusky when it could have incriminated him, with the result that the Irishman loses the woman he loves, restoring her to her husband.

The suspense is undeniably muted, though the shock appearance of the shrunken head on the bed – Milly's attempt to frighten Flusky's wife out of her wits – is a brilliantly executed moment. It is a sort of synthesis of the films of female suffering that Hitchcock seemed so preoccupied with at that time. The heroine is trying to control the household and a sinister housekeeper, as in **Rebecca**. The heroine is fighting off alcoholism and trying to reassert personality and confidence in an oppressive, distrustful household, as in **Notorious**.

As a peculiar and pondered survey of Hitchcock's favorite themes, **Under Capricorn** has some very beautiful moments, nobly enhanced by Jack Cardiff's rich photography and Richard Addinsell's romantic score.

▶ *Ingrid Bergman is terrified by the mummified human head in* **Under Capricorn** *(1949), placed there by her malicious and jealous housekeeper and suddenly illuminated by a flash of lightning. In a slow and somber film, this sudden shock moment is superbly timed.*

Misleading flashback

Hitchcock stayed in England for his next film, **Stage Fright** (1950). An aspiring actress (Jane Wyman) tries to help her boyfriend (Richard Todd), who is suspected of murder, only to discover that he is guilty all along. The limited interest of the film lies in the boyfriend's opening flashback, which turns out to be a lie (flashbacks are not usually supposed to lie) and Hitchcock's use of the theatrical background as a metaphor for role-playing and deception in real life.

The heroine suspects that the actress (Marlene Dietrich), with whom her boyfriend is infatuated, has really committed the murder. There is a clever theatrical moment when the heroine and her father (Alastair Sim) try to smoke out the actress's guilt by producing her bloodstained dress from the boyfriend's flashback: exactly like Hamlet's use of a play within a play to expose the guilt of King Claudius.

Stage Fright benefits from the potent star presences of Dietrich and Sim, the one as exotically erotic as the other is endearingly eccentric. The English humor is pleasant, like that moment when the police inspector serenades the heroine on the piano and her mother (Sybil Thorndike) clucks approvingly: "It's just like Sherlock Holmes and his fiddle."

Unfortunately, the principals are either wooden (Todd), winsome (Wyman) or wet (Wilding), and the characterization verges too much on English caricature to generate much tension. **Stage Fright** is a throwback to early Hitchcock at a time when one might have expected development more than nostalgia.

American influence

An observer of Hitchcock's development at this stage might have been a little puzzled and even dismayed at what was going on. **Rope** and **Under Capricorn** had seemed tentative attempts at breaking new ground, but had only limited success. **The Paradine Case** and **Stage Fright** seemed inferior examples of a genre Hitchcock used to do better than anyone. Questions were being raised about whether his move to America had been a beneficial or destructive influence on his work. Hitchcock was to answer such queries in the only way he knew how: a body of work of almost unbroken excellence, and even greatness, over the next decade.

Stage Fright *(1950).*
◀ *Jane Wyman in the lead part in this drama about role-playing and the conflict between appearance and reality. To help her boyfriend, who is suspected of murder, she becomes the maid to the actress who she suspects is the real guilty party.*

▼ *This film is another Hitchcock murder story with a theatrical background. Here the police watch a rehearsal while searching for the killer.*

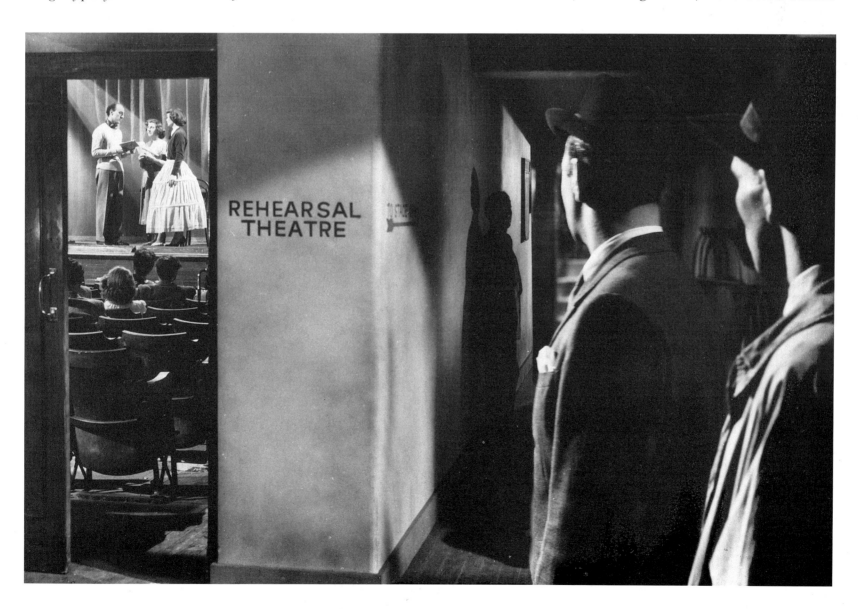

▲ *The murder attempt in* **Dial M for Murder** *(1954): Margot*

Two fundamental things happened to Alfred Hitchcock in the 1950s: he became a celebrity, and he became an artist. Both statements need some qualification and explanation. Hitchcock had always been something of a celebrity through his personal appearances in his films. And his potential as an artist had been intermittently evident in his work, though critics tended to differ in their estimation of where this artistry manifested itself – in **The 39 Steps** (1935) or **Shadow of a Doubt** (1943), in **The Lady Vanishes** (1938) or **Notorious** (1946). But in the 1950s, Hitchcock's status as celebrity and artist was made official.

Television triumphs

Celebrity status was conferred on him through his series of half-hour and hour-long playlets that appeared on American television between 1955 and 1965. There were 353 episodes, twenty of which Hitchcock personally directed. The best of these are probably the first three which he directed in 1955.

In **Breakdown**, Joseph Cotten plays a ruthless businessman paralyzed in a car crash who must break down in order to save his life: only the tears running down his cheeks while he is stretched out in the morgue show the doctors he is still alive.

In **Revenge**, Vera Miles plays a neurotic housewife who fingers a man she claims has attacked her and then, after her husband has killed him, sees another man and says: "There he is. That's him. That's him."

The Case of Mr Pelham (1955) stars Tom Ewell as a businessman whose identity and sanity are completely undermined by the sudden and inexplicable appearance of an exact double who begins to take over his life.

Perhaps the most famous Hitchcock-directed television episode, however, was **Lamb to the Slaughter** (1958), in which Barbara Bel Geddes clubs her two-timing husband to death with a chunk of frozen lamb, which she then cooks and offers to the hungry policemen while they are still vainly searching for the murder weapon.

Not only the actors but the themes of these television dramas are familiar from Hitchcock movies: madness, the extraordinary event in the ordinary setting, the duality of human personality.

What made the series so memorable was not only the stories, but the contributions of Hitchcock himself. Television made Hitchcock's profile one of the most famous in the world. His signature tune – Gounod's "Funeral March of a Marionette" – set the tone for the funereal wit of Hitchcock's prologues and epilogues to each episode, superbly written by James B. Allardyce and delivered with impeccable deadpan timing by Hitchcock himself.

When asked by Allardyce what kind of tone he wanted for his short pieces, Hitchcock offered two guidelines: his film, **The Trouble with Harry** (1955), which he had just completed; and a joke about a condemned man who on his last walk to the gallows notices the trapdoor and says apprehensively to his jailer: "I say, is that thing safe?"

Artist of anxiety

If Hitchcock's status as celebrity was conclusively established by television, his status as an artist was vigorously asserted and elevated by the polemical French critical magazine, *Cahiers du Cinéma*. For them, Hitchcock was not simply a master of suspense but an artist of anxiety on the level of Poe and Dostoevsky. He was also a Roman Catholic moralist to be talked of in the same aesthetic terms

▼ *A moment of typical Hitchcock fun in* **The Trouble With Harry** *(1955) as Edmund Gwenn tries to hide Harry's body. This moment contained Hitchcock's favorite line from all his movies. As Gwenn* *pulls the dead body by the legs as if it were a wheelbarrow, he is approached by a spinster who inquires politely: "What seems to be the trouble, Captain?"*

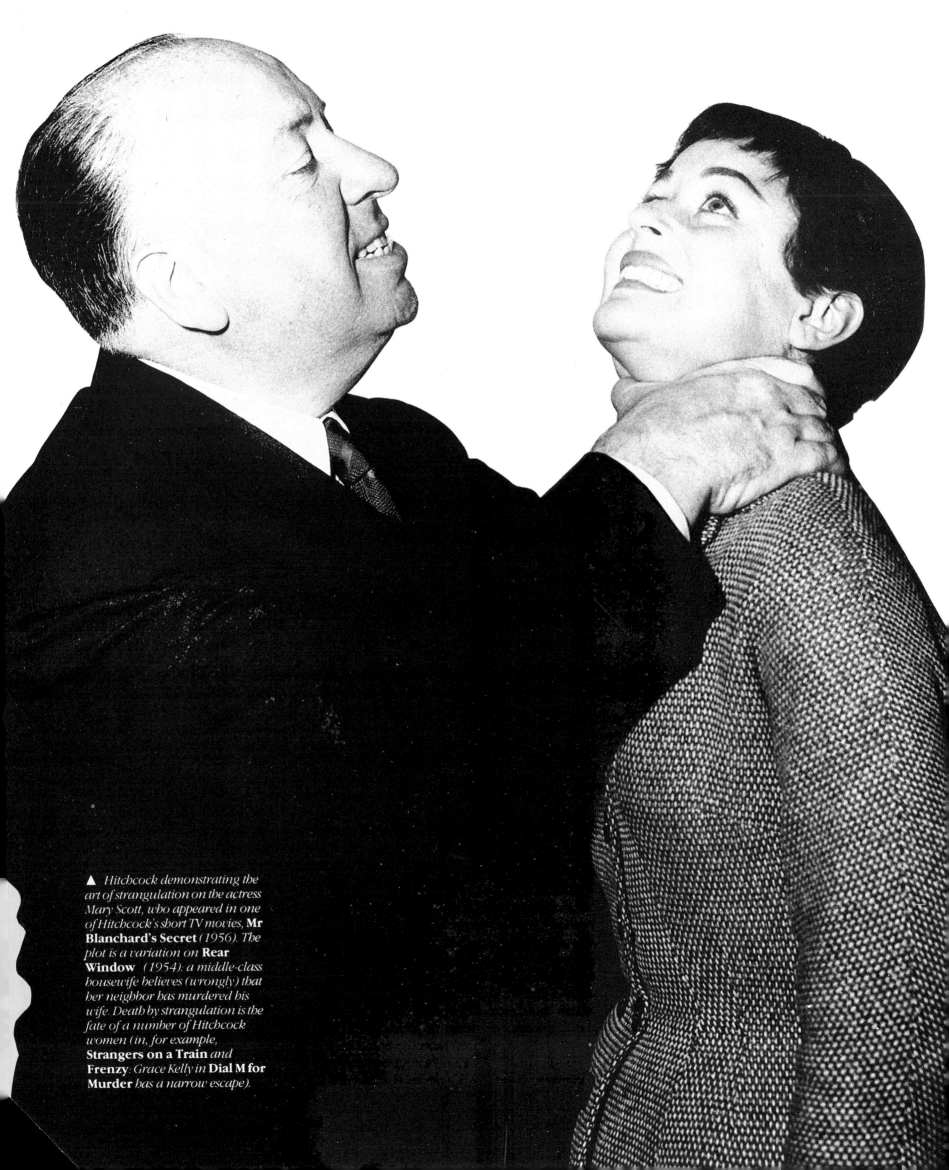

▲ *Hitchcock demonstrating the art of strangulation on the actress Mary Scott, who appeared in one of Hitchcock's short TV movies,* **Mr Blanchard's Secret** *(1956). The plot is a variation on* **Rear Window** *(1954): a middle-class housewife believes (wrongly) that her neighbor has murdered his wife. Death by strangulation is the fate of a number of Hitchcock women (in, for example,* **Strangers on a Train** *and* **Frenzy**; *Grace Kelly in* **Dial M for Murder** *has a narrow escape).*

▶ *The brilliant final set piece of* **Strangers on a Train***. A police bullet has sent a carousel careering out of control, leaving the two main characters to fight to the death. Farley Granger clings desperately onto the pole, whilst Robert Walker's foot can be seen kicking at Granger's hands and knuckles.*

as novelists like François Mauriac and Graham Greene. His films were not simply exciting melodramas, but profound studies of guilt transference, the duality of the human psyche and even of the search for God.

Such ideas were initially greeted with incredulity, even horror, by much of the British and American critical establishment. However, they were taken more seriously when Hitchcock's staunchest defenders in France – François Truffaut, Eric Rohmer and Claude Chabrol – began to develop into eminent directors themselves, much influenced by Hitchcock; and when the pro-Hitchcock critical faction, like Andrew Sarris, Robin Wood, and later Donald Spoto and William Rothman, began to argue their case with such persuasive eloquence.

Above all, the claims had to be taken seriously when Hitchcock began making films like **Rear Window** (1954), **Vertigo** (1958) and **Psycho** (1960). To deny the classic status of such intrinsically and incomparably filmic works would almost constitute a denial of cinema itself. The grounds of the argument might have changed since the 1950s, but the centrality of Hitchcock to any intelligent and informed discussion of the nature and potential of the cinema had been irrefutably established, and remains.

Return to form

Hitchcock kicked off the decade with a resounding return to form in **Strangers on a Train** (1951), adapted from Patricia Highsmith's novel. "I'm very much concerned with dualism and the good and evil that exists in everyone to some degree," said Patricia Highsmith about the novel. As we have seen, this was a fundamental concern of Hitchcock's as well.

The basic situation is dazzlingly ingenious. Two strangers, Guy (Farley Granger) and Bruno (Robert Walker), meet on a train. Each discovers that he has someone in his life he would like to be rid of – Bruno his father, Guy his clinging wife who will not give him a divorce. Bruno suggests that they swap murders: there is nothing to link the two men and therefore no motive will connect them to the murders they commit. Guy humors Bruno without taking him too seriously, but his smile vanishes when Bruno appears one night to tell him that he has murdered Guy's wife and now expects Guy to keep his side of the bargain.

Double trouble again

Although Hitchcock makes numerous changes from the novel, Highsmith's pattern of dualism is followed rigorously through the film. Bruno is clearly Guy's dark side, the literal embodiment of Guy's mental crime in wanting his wife Miriam dead. "I could strangle her," Guy shouts to his girlfriend over the phone. This is followed by the sound of a train rushing past reminding us of Guy and Bruno's meeting and the murder proposal; and then a shot of Bruno's hands which do strangle Miriam. Even prior to their meeting, we have followed the progress of both men's shoes as they cross the station; seen a shot of the railroad tracks which establishes a pattern of both crisscross and double-cross; and witnessed Hitchcock himself in his famous guest appearance trying to struggle on to a train carrying a *double*-bass.

The film invents some details to reinforce the Double theme. Guy's girlfriend, Ann (Ruth Roman), has a sister Barbara (Patricia

Hitchcock) who, in looks, is almost the double of Guy's wife and finds herself a potential murder victim of Bruno at a party ("His hands were on her throat, but he was strangling *me*").

Barbara is also like Bruno in that she says things that might be better left unsaid, because they bring subconscious desires guiltily to the surface. "Marrying the boss's daughter – short cut to a career," says Bruno of Guy's engagement to the senator's daughter: nothing in the film contradicts that. On hearing of Miriam's murder, Barbara tells Guy and Ann: "Well, you two, nothing stands in your way." True enough, and it is Bruno who has made it true.

Strangers on a Train *(1951).*
▲ *Robert Walker demonstrates the art of murder to a party guest (Norma Varden). He is watched by a disapproving Patricia Hitchcock, whose physical similarity to Walker's earlier murder victim throws Walker into a spin.*

Remarkable set-pieces

Strangers on a Train is famous for some of Hitchcock's most remarkable set-pieces. Bruno's murder of Guy's wife is shown reflected through the victim's glasses in a hideous distortion of what she had anticipated as a love scene. Guy's tennis practice is thrown when he notices that one spectator's head remains perfectly still; it is Bruno in fixed obsession gazing at Guy. There is some dazzling crosscutting between Guy's tennis match and Bruno's reaching down the grating for the incriminating lighter he has dropped, and a tremendous finale when a fight between Guy and Bruno and a careless police bullet send a carousel spinning out of control.

Unlike in the novel, Guy does not commit his murder. According to Highsmith, Hitchcock told her that he could not find a writer who could bring off the second murder, so he left it out. (One of the credited writers, novelist Raymond Chandler, did not get on with Hitchcock and found the director's idea of character "rather primitive".) Highsmith's deduction was that, "in films it would seem that the criminal has to be caught in the end in order to satisfy what is assumed to be people's sense of justice. I think this is not at all like nature, or life."

Some critics have seized on this difference to suggest Hitchcock's fundamental moral conservatism and timidity, sneering at his fear of making his hero a murderer. (A similar problem had arisen with the adaptations of **Rebecca** and **Suspicion**.) It is not that simple. In the film, Guy's refusal to go through with his end of the bargain, if anything, makes him less of a hero since it diminishes our respect. He seems as much in thrall to female figures –

passive and feeble with his bitchy wife, kept in order by the sensible and starchy Ann – as Bruno himself. As things work out, Bruno does Guy a favor from which Guy benefits but which he does not in fact repay.

How far this is deliberate and how far it is merely a consequence of Farley Granger's unsympathetic performance is hard to say. Robert Walker's witty yet anguished Bruno is an infinitely more interesting character. Is the coldness of the love scenes between Guy and Ann deliberately meant to suggest a calculated and frigid relationship, or is it just the absence of any screen chemistry between the two performers?

It is a tantalizing film, toying with complex themes of human duality, but also, in a typically Hitchcockian way, trying to wrap you up in the narrative so that you forget to ask logical questions.

The role of Guy in the film is the real ambiguity. If he is meant to be the hero, why does he not go straight away to the police when Bruno tells him of Miriam's murder? The film offers numerous explanations, but none fully discounts the most obvious: that if he did, there would be no film.

If time is of the essence in the tennis match, with Guy needing to get to the fairground to foil Bruno's attempt to frame him for the murder, why does Guy not deliberately *lose* in three quick sets, rather than play hard to win? Again, the film has some explanation for this (it reinforces the notion of Guy's ambitiousness) without entirely stifling the obvious reply: because Guy is meant to be the hero, and a hero who throws a match is both poor cinema and no longer a hero.

▼ *Guy (Farley Granger) strikes Bruno (Robert Walker) during the carousel sequence. Next to them a small boy is, in the meantime, having the time of his life. The juxtaposition of comedy and suspense is typical of Hitchcock and used very adroitly in* **Strangers on a Train***. When a film of his failed, or dissatisfied him, he would often say that "there was not enough humor in it".*

For all its excitement, **Strangers on a Train** is one of the Hitchcock films where sense and suspense do not quite go together. But the film moves with such verve and sparkle that this only belatedly becomes noticeable.

Caught in the confessional

Hitchcock followed one of his most scintillating thrillers with one of his most somber, **I Confess** (1953). The caretaker of a church in Quebec, cornered in the act of stealing, commits murder and then confesses his crime to Father Michael (Montgomery Clift). By a remarkable coincidence, the murder-victim had been threatening to blackmail the priest over a love affair the latter had prior to being ordained, and this makes the priest a prime suspect. Because of the inviolability of the confessional, he cannot reveal what the caretaker has told him and, in the eyes of the police inspector (Karl Malden), his silence only makes his guilt more likely.

"We shouldn't have made the picture," Hitchcock said later. He felt that the esoteric nature of the dilemma (the sanctity of confession) made it difficult for audiences to understand or identify with the main character. It might be, however, that Hitchcock was hurt by the failure of a film which dealt so directly with his own Catholic faith. His direction has a sense of strained earnestness and stiff reverence and is almost entirely devoid of humor.

Except in **The Wrong Man** (1956), the imagery connected with the Roman Catholic faith was to be subdued in forthcoming Hitchcock, but his basic Catholicism is revealed in his obsession with the themes of guilt, fallen man and original sin.

I Confess begins well, making dramatic use of the Quebec setting, quickly disclosing the identity of the murderer disguised in a priest's cassock, and establishing the relationship between the priest and the caretaker with great economy.

The story of the priest's love affair is eventually told by his former girlfriend (Anne Baxter) in an overlengthy but lushly filmed flashback that cleverly reflects her romanticized memory of the affair. In trying to clear Father Michael, however, the girl only implicates him further, for she provides the police with a motive. In a sense the priest is doubly betrayed, for both his former lover and his present religious loyalties seem to be inadvertently conspiring to put a noose around his neck. **I Confess** is a film of destructive relationships in which offers of help – the priest to Keller, the girl to the priest – rebound with ironic force.

Some scenes are directed with characteristic poise and punch, like the counterpointing of the banal chatter of the breakfast table with nervous camera movements that suggest the hypersensitivity of the priest and the caretaker's wife to each other's presence. At another stage, however, when the priest walks round the city in an attempt to sort out the turmoil in his mind, Hitchcock seems somewhat at a loss to find images to effectively convey Father

I Confess *(1953).*
▶ *Fr Logan (Montgomery Clift) confronts Keller (O. E. Hasse) in an early scene. The caretaker is about to confess to a murder for which the priest himself will later fall under suspicion.*

Michael's internal stress. The imagery lurches incongruously between a poster of the Humphrey Bogart film, **The Enforcer** (1951), to represent the priest's fear of arrest, and a high-angled long shot of Father Michael, with a statue of Christ carrying His cross in the foreground of the frame, to suggest the priest's burden. This latter shot is probably the one that has most encouraged the interpretation of the film as being a study of a man with a martyr complex. The priest puts little pressure on the caretaker to reveal the truth, and stoically endures the crowd's revilement of him after the trial.

Perhaps the priest's pacing the town suggests a more mundane parallel, though: the western, **High Noon** (1952), made at around the same time. **I Confess** is also a film about a man who, at whatever cost, must obey his conscience and the values by which he is pledged to live. Indeed, like **High Noon**, **I Confess** might have more to do with McCarthyism than Catholicism. It is about a man of principle, standing alone against the mob, who nevertheless refuses to testify simply to save his own skin.

▼ *Brian Aherne cross-examines Montgomery Clift during the trial scene. Clift is examining the cassock, worn as a disguise by the real murderer, which seems to implicate the priest still further. The visual prominence given to the figure of the crucified Christ on the wall is one of several such moments which made* **I Confess** *one of Hitchcock's most overtly religious films, often interpreted as a film about the temptation of martyrdom.*

Purgatory

Hitchcock's next film, **Dial M for Murder** (1954), was, in his own words, a means of recharging the batteries and of experimenting with 3-D (which had gone out of fashion by the time of the film's release, so that it was shown in a normal version). Based on Frederick Knott's highly successful play, **Dial M for Murder** concerns a husband's elaborate attempt to murder his adulterous wife. When the scheme backfires and she kills her assailant, he almost succeeds in framing her for murder.

"I didn't need to go into the studio," Hitchcock said of the film,

Dial M for Murder *(1954).*
▼ *The prospective murderer (Anthony Dawson) waits for his victim, played by Grace Kelly. The ringing phone signals that her husband's murder plan is now in action.*

▶*Here playboy Ray Milland checks that hired assassin Anthony Dawson is really dead, while the intended victim, Grace Kelly, looks on. Now he has to think of another way to murder his unfaithful wife.*

"I could have phoned that one in." Although it is a minor work, it is not as negligible as Hitchcock would imply. He could still do more with tiny details of hands, shadows, keys than most directors could manage with wide-screen spectacle, which was the popular fashion of the time.

He also always had the gift of being able to film dialogue so that an audience would hang on every word, often teasing them along with an unorthodox camera angle. Particularly memorable in this film is the overhead shot of the apartment as the husband (Ray Milland) takes his accomplice over his murder plan like a general explaining strategy over a map. There is, also, the perversely playful shot of the inner workings of a phone as the husband inserts the coin for the call which he intends will lead to the death of his wife.

What intensifies the film is the situation of the wife. It was Hitchcock's first film with Grace Kelly, the archetypal ice-cool blonde of whom Hitchcock would become enamored in his movies and whom he would thaw through the sadistic expedient of putting them through purgatorial fire. Her two kisses which begin the picture (of her husband, then of her lover) establish the wife's deceptiveness and betrayal with brutal directness, almost as if to justify the punishment of her that follows.

A sinister, semi-circular movement of the camera behind her back as she talks on the phone anticipates imminent murderous assault. Accusing looks impale her on an altar of guilt and vulnerability as the circumstantial evidence against her mounts. Her trial is filmed entirely through close-ups, with colored lights revolving around her against a natural background. The close-ups avoid dissipating the tension while the changing colors suggest her purgatorial experience. Hitchcock's heroines are photographed ravishingly but undergo terrible ordeals, as the price that must be paid for their beauty.

Curiously, murdered wives were to become an obsession of Hitchcock's films of the 1950s (**Strangers on a Train**, **I Confess**, **Dial M for Murder**, **Rear Window**, **Vertigo** all contain the theme) and, equally oddly, the names of the menaced or murdered heroines of **Strangers on a Train**, **Dial M for Murder**, **Vertigo**, **Psycho**, **The Birds** and **Marnie** all begin with the letter 'M'. (Coincidentally, Hitchcock always referred to his wife, Alma Reville, as "Madame".) "Dial M for Misogyny" might be a more appropriate title.

Helpless witness

Dial M for Murder might have been little more than a mechanical exercise for Hitchcock, but his next film, **Rear Window** (1954), showed him with all creative energies at full stretch. Without question his best film since **Notorious**, it won Hitchcock his third Oscar nomination as director and is a work that goes to the heart of the method and meaning of Hitchcockian cinema.

Immobilized in a chair after an accident, a magazine photographer (James Stewart) passes the time by looking through binoculars at the events in the apartment block opposite. Slowly he begins to suspect that one of the occupants (Raymond Burr) might have murdered his wife. The remainder of the film is concerned with the photographer's attempt to persuade his girlfriend (Grace Kelly), his nurse (Thelma Ritter) and his policeman friend (Wendell Corey) of the validity of his suspicions, and what happens when the murderer opposite becomes aware that Stewart knows his guilty secret.

Powerful montage

The triumph of the film is its ability to operate on many levels. For Hitchcock, it was the opportunity to show the power of film and to demonstrate how you can create something galvanizingly cinematic entirely through montage from a situation that is essentially static.

"For example," said Hitchcock, "let's say Mr Stewart is looking out into this courtyard and – let's say – he sees a woman with a child in her arms. Well, the first cut is Mr Stewart, then what he sees, and then his reaction. We'll see him smile. Now if you took away the center piece of film and substituted – we'll say – a shot of the girl Miss Torso in a bikini, instead of being a benevolent gentleman he's now a dirty old man. And you've only changed one piece of film, you haven't changed his look, or his reaction . . . It's the piecing together of the montage which makes what I call a pure film."

Rear Window is constructed entirely on this montage principle and is as exciting a piece of film as one could see. It needs a fine actor to help sustain it, of course, and James Stewart gives one of the great cinematic performances in which the eyes are as eloquent and expressive as the words.

Disturbing moral tone

It is not only the method that is quintessential Hitchcock. There is also the disturbing moral tone. After all, Stewart is a Peeping Tom: can one entirely endorse his behavior? There is a suggestion that he almost wills the man opposite into becoming a murderer, in order to brighten up his own temporarily boring existence, and is then compelled to live through the consequences of his impure emotions when the murderer turns on him. If you like, it is a nice little metaphor for the experience of watching a Hitchcock film. How many audiences at **The Birds** (1963) have got a little impatient with Hitchcock's measured opening and hoped for and almost willed the bird attacks, only to be discomfited by their severity when they do come?

Rear Window has often been seen as an allegory of the filmgoing experience, with the block of flats opposite standing for the cinema screen and with Stewart being a sort of filmgoer, who pro-

Rear Window *(1954).*
◄ *Raymond Burr as the murderer. A picture has been built up of the murderer as a monster but when he confronts Stewart at close quarters he seems a bewildered, pathetic, vulnerable figure. "What do you want of me?" he asks Stewart. The answer is, basically: excitement to enliven a dull convalescence.*

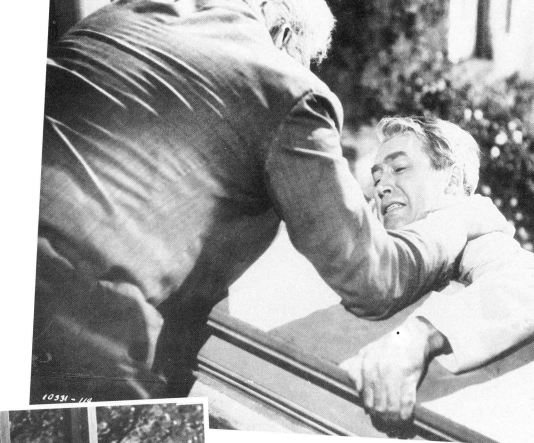

▼ The struggle between Raymond Burr and James Stewart. Stewart has tried to keep his attacker at bay by dazzling him with his flashbulbs. Now, ▶ like so many Hitchcock characters, he must cling on for dear life to avoid falling to his death. This image from near the end of the film interestingly foreshadows the opening sequence of the subsequent **Vertigo** *(1958), where Stewart is once again dangling over a precipice.*

jects his own fantasies on to the characters he sees, identifying with some, rejecting others, but above all yearning for them to provide him with excitement.

But there are other dimensions as well. The whole situation in **Rear Window** of spying on neighbors might have had uncomfortable resonances in McCarthyist America, with its atmosphere of paranoia and betrayal. What Stewart sees also begins to form a portrait of his own character. What binds his vision together particularly is his subconscious fear of marriage. It is established that he is uncertain whether or not to marry his girlfriend – whether bachelorhood means freedom or loneliness, whether marriage means harmony or chains.

What he sees in that apartment block can be read as a kind of selective, intense, almost hallucinatory projection of his own sexual anxiety. A girl waiting for her husband contrasts with another character he calls "Miss Lonelyhearts". A couple of newlyweds contrasts with the man he suspects has chopped his wife into little pieces. What he sees, in other words, is frustrated love, displaced love, fantasy compensations for the absence of love, love that is new and love that has turned to hate.

His obsessive voyeurism is a way of postponing the day when he must look into the window of his own soul and ask what it is *he* wants. "If you could only see yourself," as his nurse says, with unconscious irony.

Rear Window is vintage Hitchcock, about cinema, character, manipulation and emotion, lenses and loneliness. The soundtrack is exquisitely composed, and John Michael Hayes's screenplay has a clever wit and structure that brilliantly complements Hitchcock's misanthropic view of the Human Comedy.

Style without substance

After the achievement of **Rear Window**, Hitchcock understandably relaxed, and his next movie, **To Catch a Thief** (1955), is one of his most lightweight. Cary Grant plays a retired jewel thief living in France who becomes chief suspect when a series of jewelry thefts in the area seem to bear his signature. He deploys his former gifts to trap the real culprit.

It is a stylish film without much substance. Robert Burks won a well-merited Oscar for his photography, which manages to be tense and touristy at the same time (as in an early car chase photographed from helicopter height so one can simultaneously admire the scenery).

Cary Grant plays with great style and Grace Kelly smolders beautifully. A love scene crosscut with shots of soundless fireworks is erotically suggestive without a hint of visual impropriety.

With its lush settings, its wit, its climactic fancy dress ball and its jewelry, **To Catch a Thief** might well have been a substantial influence on Blake Edwards' **The Pink Panther** (1963). It is deftly done in a rather detached manner. Only in the final sequence, when the real thief is unmasked, does Hitchcock generate his usual suspense through atmospheric camera movement: the slow track from Grant as he waits tensely on the roof, and then the sudden fast pan as Grant realizes he is not alone.

Eccentric and offbeat

Hitchcock's next film, **The Trouble with Harry** (1955), is one of his most eccentric and offbeat. A personal favorite of his own, it did not find an immediate audience. Delicate autumnal shades frame a lot of worrying over Harry, who is a corpse seen only in a series of foreshortened shots of his shoes and then socks. A number of people might have killed him, and the body proves remarkably difficult to dispose of. The film flirts with the themes of sex and death

11511-14

To Catch a Thief *(1955).*
◄ *A romantic moment for socialite (Grace Kelly) and reformed robber (Cary Grant).*

▲ *The fireworks are about to begin as Grace Kelly tempts Cary Grant with her jewels. "Here, hold them... they're the most beautiful thing in the world, the one thing you can't resist," she says provocatively as she draws him into a close embrace. It's unlikely that she's referring only to her diamonds.*

Overleaf: Cat burglar on a hot tin roof. As the fancy dress ball spills out onto the terrace, Cary Grant is spotted on the roof, which seems to confirm his guilt as the jewel thief. But somebody else is on the roof with him. The suspenseful denouement of an otherwise relaxed film.

in the manner of American Puritan literature, but it also has a very English delight in the mirthfully macabre (it is based on a novel by English writer Jack Trevor Story).

There is much charm in the playing of Shirley MacLaine, John Forsythe, Edmund Gwenn and Mildred Natwick, and just when the film is sacrificing tension for talk, a new little twist in the plot sets things going again.

It is brilliantly scored by Bernard Herrmann in his most tender and puckish mood. The tone is like that of Hitchcock in his TV shows, more sardonic than suspenseful, perhaps too idiosyncratic finally to command a large following, but a pleasure, nonetheless. It is significant, however, as Hitchcock's first collaboration with Herrmann, with whom, on his next seven films, he was to form one of the greatest director/composer partnerships in the history of the movies.

One and only remake

With his following film, **The Man Who Knew Too Much** (1956), Hitchcock for the only time in his career remade an earlier success. It was a controversial decision, since it reopened the debate about the superiority or otherwise of Hitchcock's American films to his earlier English ones, and whether Hitchcock's career had become more profound or simply more ponderous.

Hitchcock felt that "the first version is the work of a talented amateur and the second was made by a professional." Although many British critics in particular prefer the 1934 version, the second is infinitely better. It is much longer than the original (120 minutes as opposed to 75) but, because of the superiority of the acting, direction, characterization and overall technical excellence, time passes much more quickly.

The man who knows too much is an American doctor, played by James Stewart. On holiday in Morocco with his wife (Doris Day) he inadvertently witnesses a murder in a market and becomes privy to a plot of political assassination. This is being masterminded by an ostensibly "stick in the mud" English couple (Bernard Miles and Brenda de Banzie) they have met in a restaurant, and is due to take place in London in a few days' time. In order to prevent Stewart from going to the police, the couple kidnap his son.

Like **Rear Window**, the film is about marriage as well as murder. Stewart is a man who knows too much, in another sense: a know-all, whose posture of male supremacy and dominance (he has compelled his wife to give up her singing career) is gradually undermined by events. It is his wife who is more observant of the sinister developments in Morocco. It is she who recognizes that the name "Ambrose Chapel" whispered in Stewart's ear is not a person but a place, and who plays a crucial role in foiling the assassination plot.

Stewart is reduced to relatively ignoble actions. He deliberately sedates his wife to subdue her reaction to the news of their son's kidnap (a powerful and uncomfortable scene). He partakes in a wild goose chase in a taxidermist's (a delightful diversion in the film). And he is trapped in and has to climb out of a chapel on the rope of a bell tower, an intriguing anticipation of **Vertigo**. This self-important and domineering man merely thrashes around on the outskirts of the plot, finally being made forcibly aware of his own limitations and of the capabilities of other people, especially his wife, whom he has greatly underestimated.

Menace and manners

The opening section in Morocco is a gripping blend of menace and

The Man Who Knew Too Much (1956).
▶ *James Stewart is about to be overpowered. With the help of his wife, he has managed to trace his son's kidnapper (Bernard Miles, standing behind Stewart) to the Ambrose Chapel, but his search again leads to a frustrating conclusion. Eventually his wife foils the assassination plot and instigates the recovery of their son.*

▼ *The kidnap victim (Christopher Olsen) is forced downstairs at gunpoint.*

manners, Hitchcock proving as adroit an observer of marital strain and social etiquette as of the more melodramatic aspects of the thriller plot.

The film's greatest scene is the assassination attempt at the Royal Albert Hall, timed to coincide with a cymbal clash during the performance of Benjamin's "Storm Cloud Cantata" that will cover the sound of the shot. The suspense is conveyed through color (the red curtains of the assassin's theater box, the cymbals on the red chairs); visual symmetry (the similarity in appearance of the unsuspecting cymbalist and the equally unsuspecting target) and by a stretching of the time factor: we know what will trigger the attempt but we do not know in advance where the cymbal clash occurs.

After that sequence, the film runs down, affording a resolution to the plot, and the opportunity for Doris Day to sing her big hit "Que Sera Sera" (which is integrated cleverly into the drama of the film despite the banality of the lyrics and melody – by Ray Evans and Jay Livingston). Perhaps because the plot is essentially a red herring to explore the tensions in the marriage, the film seems a little less concentrated than the very best Hitchcock.

Victimized hero

Hitchcock next made one of his most serious films. **The Wrong Man** (1956) tells the true story of musician Manny Balestrero (Henry Fonda) who, through a case of mistaken identity, is arrested for a crime he did not commit and, through a chain of circumstantial evidence, is unable to prove his innocence. Although he bears his misfortune with fortitude, the strain proves too much for his wife (Vera Miles) who feels that Manny is being punished for her failures in the marriage, and herself becomes buried under a landslide of fear and guilt.

The theme of "the wrong man" had been dealt with before in Hitchcock, but never with the documentary sobriety of this film. More than any other Hitchcock movie, **The Wrong Man** projects his fear of and hostility toward the police. Much more than Orson Welles's film of **The Trial** (1962), it has a Kafkaesque sense of the nightmarish processes of the law whereby "without doing anything wrong", an innocent man can suddenly have his life arbitrarily turned upside down.

It is the Hitchcock film that is closest to Fritz Lang, with its casting of Henry Fonda as the victimized hero (as in Lang's **You Only Live Once**, 1937), with its image of the city as a prison – all steel, harsh shadow and straight lines – and with its terrifying sense of the remorseless power of Fate. In her scene with the psychiatrist, Vera Miles as the wife sounds almost like the murderer (Peter Lorre) in Lang's **M** (1931). "They wanted to punish me because I'd failed him, let him down . . ." she says. "They come at me from all sides . . . They know I'm guilty."

The Wrong Man *(1956).*
◄ *Manny (Henry Fonda) tries to comfort his wife (Vera Miles) during the onset of their misfortunes.*

◀ *After a night in jail, Manny (Henry Fonda) is brought before a hearing to set the date of his trial. Standing on Fonda's left is Charles Cooper, playing one of the chief detectives. Seated between them is Manny's brother-in-law (Nehemiah Persoff), who puts up the bail to bring the nightmare to a temporary concluion.*

▼ *During the long night of her husband's arrest, Vera Miles rings round frantically trying to find out what has happened to him. Her mother-in-law (Esther Minciotti) shares her anxiety. Meanwhile at the police station, when the accused man inquires whether his wife has been informed, the policemen reply with curt dishonesty: "That's been taken care of". Their callousness adds to the disquieting suspense of these family scenes.*

Stripped of identity

The first half of the film is unrelentingly oppressive. The nightmare begins from the moment when Balestrero enters the insurance office and a clerk mistakenly recognizes him as one who robbed the office a week before. The tension is screwed up tight by her terrified look as he reaches in his pocket for the insurance policy, and also by another girl's furtive glance at the unwitting suspect over a colleague's shoulder.

With its hollow reassurances, false promises and clinical coldness, police procedure strips Balestrero of his identity. The locking of the handcuffs is a further stage in his humiliation. Hitchcock's point-of-view shots here of legs and feet convey the hero's feelings of depression and defeat through his inability to look up. When bail is put up and he is released from prison, one can almost feel the fresh air on his cheeks.

Because it is less claustrophobic, the second half of the film has not the same intensity, but it remains absorbing drama. The wife's growing mental illness is first revealed in a scene with the lawyer, in which the routine dialogue is counterpointed by uncomfortable and edgy camerawork directed towards the wife's disturbing detachment. It is one of those scenes Hitchcock does so well, where the camera tells the story and the dialogue is just atmosphere and hardly important. A smashed mirror in an argument with her husband foreshadows her own sense of fractured identity and her eventual psychological breakdown.

Tragedy and waste

The turning-point occurs when Manny prays for strength. Great visual emphasis has been given to his clutching of his rosary beads during his trial. Now when Manny prays, Hitchcock slowly dissolves to a shot of a man walking towards the foreground of the frame and into close-up. It is the guilty man, "miraculously" about to commit another crime which will clear Balestrero's name. Small wonder that those French critics who stress Hitchcock as a religious artist give particular emphasis to that moment. As Truffaut suggested to Hitchcock, one cannot imagine anyone but a Catholic handling that scene in quite that way.

Nevertheless, the "miracle" is not complete. Balestrero's free-dom was taken away by a look ("just look at him," the clerk was instructed). It is entirely appropriate that he should reassert his identity with an emphatic look at the guilty man. But, in the final scene with his wife at the hospital, Rose can only respond wanly to the news with the words, "That's fine for *you*."

"I guess I was hoping for a miracle," Balestrero says, and the nurse points out: "She's not listening now."

Although an end title assures us (perhaps untruthfully) that the wife made a full recovery, the film leaves us with a sense of tragedy and waste. It is one of Hitchcock's most thoughtful essays on the fragility of identity and the precariousness of our supposedly ordered existence.

◄ *The grim secret of the cellar in* **Psycho** *(1960), or the image of American Motherhood. Having made her son Norman in her own image, Mrs Bates suffers the consequences: murder at his hands and preservation by taxidermy.*

The five films Hitchcock made between 1958 and 1964 represent the pinnacle of his achievement. They are the American equivalent of his British sextet of 1934-38, with which he confirmed his reputation as the country's greatest film-maker. They may not all be among Hitchcock's five best films, though three of them are (**Vertigo**, **Psycho** and **The Birds**) and the other two (**North by Northwest** and **Marnie**) surely belong in the top ten. Together they take to the furthest point certain developments of theme and style that Hitchcock had been refining through the years. Within the familiar suspense framework they are bold, experimental, innovatory films that take risks which, astonishingly, nearly all come off.

Narrative originality

What is it about these films that makes them special even in the context of Hitchcock's preceding work? The immediately noticeable thing is their narrative originality. Each of the five films has some peculiarity or idiosyncrasy, either in its story or the way the story is told.

Vertigo (1958) has three such oddities. It gets away with murder. It gives away its "surprise" ending two-thirds of the way through. The actual ending is left standing on a precarious tightrope of triumph and trauma.

North by Northwest (1959) has a plot that is almost impossible to paraphrase, since eccentrically violent events keep occurring to a character who cannot account for them. (When Cary Grant complained to Hitchcock that "we've already done a third of the picture and I still can't make head or tail of it," Hitchcock pointed out to him that he was using a line of his own dialogue.)

The narrative structures of **Psycho** (1960) and **The Birds** (1963) are so original that they were profoundly influential. Their slow build-up of suspense, in which nothing happens yet the audience is being carefully conditioned, was to be consciously copied by the 1973 horror movie, **The Exorcist**. The exploitation of audience identification, in order to heighten the impact when the film takes off, had a significant effect on the structure of the gangster classic, **Bonnie and Clyde** (1967).

When Hitchcock kills his heroine a third of the way through **Psycho**, he violates audiences' belief that a film will never arbitrarily bump off its star. From this time forward, movie audiences will never be as secure again. **The Birds** ends on an uneasy truce, with no explanation: it is a remarkable gauntlet thrown down to the mass audience's usual demand for final clarification. **Marnie** has an ambiguous ending that follows Hitchcock's strangest, most stylized flashback.

In some ways it is hardly appropriate to talk about plot in relation to these films, for they proceed through theme, motif and tone. They are closer to the way poetry and music operate on our emotions than the novel or drama. One might add that it is often the case in Hitchcock that, the more outrageous the plot, the more perceptive, provocative and profound the psychology.

Psychological disorder

Corresponding to the narrative originality is the thematic intensity. **Vertigo** and **Marnie** are the ultimate Hitchcock studies of psychological disorder, involving romantic obsession in the former case and a Freudian case-history in the latter, and in both films taken to a new pitch of psychosexual agony.

North by Northwest is Hitchcock's most extreme vision of political paranoia, his most elaborate double-chase extravaganza, and his most extensive tour across the physical, symbolic and psychological landscape of America.

Both **Psycho** and **The Birds** take Hitchcock's favorite theme of the eruption of chaos into the world of order to such a degree of terror that both become not simply suspense films but horror films. Hitchcock has always played with audience expectations, but **Psycho** is his coldest and cruelest manipulation of them. Hitchcock has always been grimly humorous about the blandness of bourgeois life and has always disdained plausibility in his films, but **The Birds** is his most savage assault on bourgeois values and his most extreme denial that reason is the foundation of certainty in knowledge.

This quintet of films also brings to a climax Hitchcock's treatment of sexual relationships. As we have seen, the fears and fantasies, anxieties and unease that have surfaced in Hitchcock's treatment of sexual attraction generate a profoundly disturbing tension in which feelings fluctuate violently between love and hate.

"I may go back to hating you," says Cary Grant to Eva Marie Saint in **North by Northwest**, "it was more fun."

In many ways, the main source of suspense in Hitchcock is sex, and, in these films, the bizarre sexual hang-ups of the characters are exposed and analyzed with a boldness rare in the popular cinema. In the men, the sexual disorders range from necrophilia in **Vertigo**, transvestism in **Psycho**, to fetishism in **Marnie**. In the females, they range from suggestions of nymphomania in **North by Northwest**, and promiscuity in **Psycho**, to frustration in **The Birds** and frigidity in **Marnie**.

What this amounts to is an explosive critical blast at the place of heterosexual love in our society and a questioning of the centrality of the family. In all of these films, the family is incomplete or inadequate in some way. Father figures are absent, and clinging or possessive mothers figure in **North by Northwest, The Birds** and, particularly, in **Psycho** and **Marnie**. What these films propose is wholesale condemnation of matriarchal America. A remarkable set of films, then, as suspenseful and entertaining as the best of Hitchcock, but with this additional technical and structural boldness.

Visions of death

Vertigo begins more or less where **Rear Window** (1954) left off. At the end of the earlier film, James Stewart had both legs in plaster, having been pushed out of his apartment window by a murderer. In the opening scene of **Vertigo**, Stewart, then a police detective, is seen clinging to a collapsing gutter. He hangs on, but a policeman who tries to help him falls to his death and the vertiginous vision of death that the hero has faced irreparably alters his perspective on life.

Vertigo takes to the point of tragedy what **Rear Window** kept in the realm of misanthropic suspense comedy: namely, the hero's sexual anxiety which in **Rear Window** took the form of curiosity and voyeurism and in **Vertigo** becomes a morbid obsession with necrophilia.

James Stewart plays Scottie Ferguson, now a private detective, who is hired by an old schoolfriend, Gavin Elster (Tom Helmore), to shadow Elster's wife, Madeleine (Kim Novak). Elster thinks that his wife is possessed by the spirit of an ancestor, Carlotta Valdes,

Vertigo *(1958).*

◀ *Chasing a criminal across the rooftops of San Francisco, Scottie (James Stewart) slips and has to cling to the grating, in the process discovering his terrible fear of heights. One never sees how he got down and it is hard to imagine how he could. He remains a character on the edge, in vertiginous suspension, for the rest of the film.*

▲ *Trailing his client's wife, who seems obsessed by the memory of an ancestor who killed herself, James Stewart is shocked to see the lady (Kim Novak) throw herself into San Francisco Bay. Here he rescues her and carries her to his car.*

who committed suicide and he fears that some harm will come to Madeleine. She does indeed throw herself, trance-like, into San Francisco Bay, and in rescuing her and coming to know her, Scottie falls in love. Later, however, still apparently "possessed", she rushes to the top of a mission church tower, Scottie's vertigo prevents him from following and he sees her fall to her death. The tragedy precipitates his complete nervous breakdown.

On recovery, he seems to project an image of Madeleine on to every woman he encounters. In one case, he is so struck by a likeness that he follows the girl, Judy, back to her hotel room and asks her to dinner. We move into the final phase: the revelation that Judy and the woman who Scottie thought was Madeleine are one and the same. Scottie has been the dupe in an elaborate plot by Elster to murder his real wife. Scottie's delirious attempt to transform Judy back into Madeleine will not re-create an illusion but will shatter it.

Intriguing minor details

Like Billy Wilder's film, **Fedora** (1978), which shares a lot of the preoccupations of the Hitchcock work, **Vertigo** is one of those movies which gets better rather than weaker once one knows the central twist of the plot. It becomes possible to notice ironies, nuances and double-meanings in phrases and looks that were not originally spotted: "I'm not mad, I'm not mad," cries Madeleine to Scottie in their scene on the rocks: it seems a cry of despair from a possessed woman, but, in retrospect, the line could mean, "I'm not Madeleine," from an actress, Judy, who is becoming increasingly uncomfortable with her role.

"No one possesses you, you're safe with me," Scottie tells Madeleine. But later in the film, he attempts to possess Judy and she is anything but safe.

Elster, comforting Scottie at the inquest, says: "You and I know who killed Madeleine." At the time it seems a compassionate acknowledgment that the spirit of the dead Carlotta was responsible for Madeleine's death, not Scottie. At the end, the line has a very different resonance: Scottie and Elster know who killed Madeleine but they will remain the only two people who will ever know – *only* "you and I".

This is one of the intriguing minor details of **Vertigo** which escaped the Hollywood censors: a story of the perfect murder in which the villain gets away scot-free. But to describe **Vertigo** purely on the level of plot is to give no real impression of how the film works. Indeed, Hitchcock more or less ditches narrative plausibility at a very early stage – in the scene when the detective follows Madeleine to a hotel only to find undeniable evidence that she cannot have been there. From that point, the film proceeds like a dream-like poem on the theme of romantic illusion, in which the hero is "half in love with easeful death".

Labyrinthine pursuit

The early part of the film follows the detective's labyrinthine pursuit of the mysterious Madeleine from behind the wheel of his car. Slowly a cluster of images begins to form around Madeleine's obsession with Carlotta (and Scottie's obsession with Madeleine): flowers, trees, a necklace, the sea, the church. Recurring images of dark corridors and an open grave seem about to swallow up all the main characters in darkness. The overhead shot of Scottie descending the dark stairs after Madeleine's death has a sense of a descent into hell, and the subjective shots of his vertigo spasms (achieved by a combination of tracking shot and forward zoom) convey a terrifying impression of both a fear of falling and yet a yearning for oblivion.

Visually, the film is dominated by circles and spirals. Even Madeleine's hair is caught in a tight little coil at the back of her head and the setting of San Francisco, with its twists and turns, heights and dips, seems indispensable to the drama. The plot, too, goes round in dizzying circles. A policeman falls at the beginning of the film, the real Madeleine in the middle, Judy at the end. Madeleine is possessed by the past and this leads to Scottie's similar possession by the past after her death ("Do you believe that someone out of the past, someone dead, can enter and take possession of a living being?" Elster has asked Scottie ironically in their first meeting). In trying to "make over" Judy into Madeleine by forcing her to wear the same clothes and change her appearance, Scottie unwittingly re-creates the very process by which Elster deceived and ensnared him in the first place.

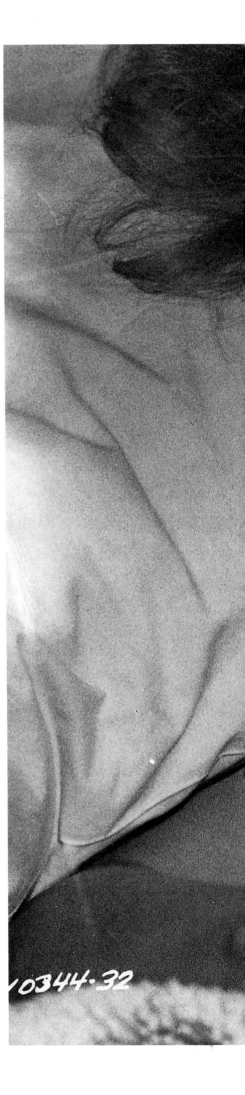

Vertigo (1958).
▶ *Madeleine (Kim Novak) wakes up after her suicide attempt and suddenly realizes that Scottie has had to undress her to remove her wet clothing. The following scene between them is full of stirrings of delicate longing and sexual tension.*

Vertigo (1958).

▲ In a state of trauma, Scottie (James Stewart) descends the stairs of the bell-tower having seen the woman he loves fall to her death – or so he thinks. Later he is struck by a discrepancy – the body he saw falling past the window looked dead and yet he heard a scream. At this particular moment, however, he is preoccupied with his loss: the shot wonderfully conveys his oppressive sense of guilt and grief and the depths of despair into which he sinks.

◄ Two wanderers find each other. Scottie (James Stewart) finds himself falling in love with Madeleine (Kim Novak).

► *Kim Novak as the "double", whom James Stewart remakes in the image of the woman he loved, little realizing that these women are one and the same. Hitchcock called the transformation scene "striptease in reverse".*

▼ *Judy (Kim Novak) disguised as Madeleine screams as the murderer (Tom Helmore) prepares to throw his wife's dead body off the top of the bell tower. Yet how did he get her up there in the first place?* **Vertigo** *defies such logical questions. The moment is part of Novak's extraordinary flashback in which the film's surprise ending is revealed two-thirds of the way through.*

10344-58

Most audacious film

All this is intensified by a quite extraordinary visual style. Long before the end, Hitchcock has left realism and even heightened suspense far behind. Stylistically it is his most audacious film because it includes elements of the Gothic and of the surreal. The imagery of towers and open graves and the themes of wandering ghosts and demonic possession recall the American Gothicism of Poe and Henry James. **Vertigo**'s atmosphere of dream and its theme of the mad extremities of love evoke the world of surrealism.

Scottie's nightmare leading to his breakdown is a particular example of a surrealist use of heightened unreality to convey emotional excess. The scene is a remarkable combination of image, music, color and even animation. The bold, stylistic artificiality of the nightmare implies a nagging doubt in Scottie's mind about the truth of what he has been through.

Most remarkable of all is the love scene between Scottie and Judy. When Judy is finally transformed into a mirror image of Madeleine, Hitchcock suffuses the screen in a sickly shade of green – romantic dementia and masculine dominance taken to the point of near-nausea. The long kiss that follows is done in a 360-degree panning shot against which Hitchcock backprojects the livery stable where Scottie and Madeleine first acknowledged their love. It is Scottie's re-creation of the past, the triumph of his romantic illusion which, by the very fact that it seems *too* identical, too perfect, again begins to plant seeds of anxiety in his mind.

Bernard Herrmann's music, which is magnificent throughout, is especially intelligent here. His love theme, which seems consciously and appropriately to echo Wagner's "Liebestod" from *Tristan and Isolde*, strives for a romantic climax without quite being able to sustain it, and the scene ends on a diminuendo of doubt. The stage is set for the terrifying finale in which Scottie discovers the grand deception and brutally takes Judy through the crime again. This temptation of the perversities of Providence is climaxed by a repeat of the earlier fall and a staggering final shot of Scottie at the top of the tower, looking down and stretching out his arms, cured yet destroyed, released yet desolate, possibly poised to jump.

Tributes all round

One could not leave **Vertigo** without extolling James Stewart's astonishing performance, a study of disturbed romantic obsession wellnigh unmatched in the cinema. He is magnificently supported by Barbara Bel Geddes as Scottie's friend, Midge, the epitome of honest, down-to-earth maternal womanhood in Scottie's eyes. And by Kim Novak as Madeleine/Judy, representing in his eyes the sensual mystery of woman and a more visionary dimension of life.

Hitchcock was allegedly unhappy about Miss Novak's performance and had originally cast Vera Miles in the role until she had had the temerity to become pregnant. But, in this case, presence is more important than performance, and Miss Novak's glamorous unreality in the role now seems perfect.

From a group of tortured characters clinging tenuously to their fragile illusions and sense of identity, Hitchcock has fashioned a film of genuine tragedy, mad power and cinematic genius. **Vertigo** is a passionate film, but also a compassionate one, disclosed particularly in the very last line: "God have mercy . . . "

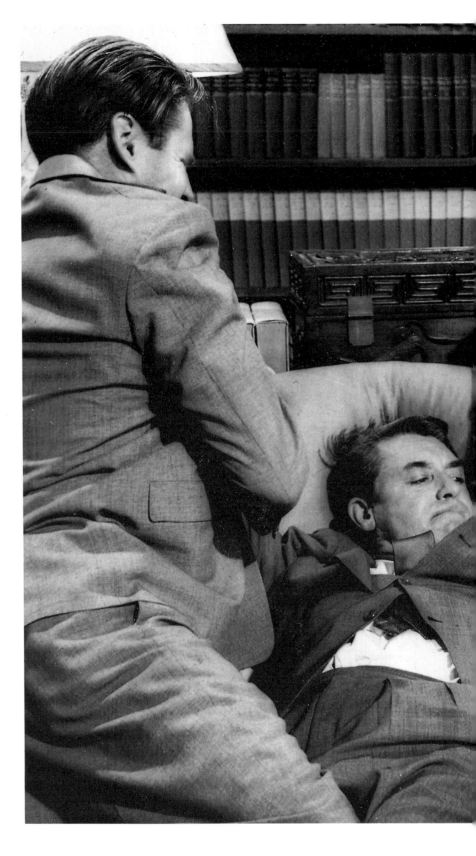

▲ *Mistaken for a spy in* **North by Northwest** *(1959), Roger (Cary Grant) is force-fed neat bourbon to facilitate the arrangement for his "accidental" death. Martin Landau is pouring the hefty drink; Adam Williams (left) and Robert Ellenstein (right) hold him down.*

No laughing matter

"It's so horribly sad," says a CIA man in **North by Northwest**, "how is it I feel like laughing?" It is a question one might ask of the film. Hitchcock's first movie after **Vertigo** might also have its serious implications about identity and sexual tensions, but they are kept at arm's length by the sheer delight in malevolent inventiveness. Hitchcock often recalled remarking at story conferences: "Wouldn't it be fun if we killed him this way?" **North by Northwest** remains the greatest of all comedy thrillers precisely because of its ability to be at its funniest when also at its most frightening.

Along with the scripts for **Shadow of a Doubt** and **Rear Window**, Ernest Lehman's screenplay for **North by Northwest** is probably the best Hitchcock ever had. Some measure of its quality can be gauged from the number of times it has been imitated – as, for example, by Lehman himself in his screenplay for Mark Robson's **The Prize** (1963) and by Michelangelo Antonioni in his film **The Passenger** (1975).

The basic situation is delightfully outrageous. An advertising man, Roger O. Thornhill (Cary Grant), is mistaken for a secret agent and threatened and chased across the length and breadth of America. What sharpens the situation is the impeccable logic by which this absurd premise is developed, and the wit and wisdom of the dialogue.

On the train, when Thornhill gives a false name to the mysterious lady (Eva Marie Saint) who seems to have picked him up, she immediately puts him in his place: "You're Roger Thornhill of Madison Avenue and you're wanted for murder on every front page in America – *don't* be so modest."

When Thornhill is rescued from the police by the Professor (Leo G. Carroll) and asks him whom he works for, the Professor replies: "F.B.I., C.I.A. – we're all part of the same alphabet soup." The sinister, secretive, self-serving stew of international politics has never been more succinctly expressed.

Anything but bovine

Cary Grant has been taken too much for granted. As the hollow advertising man (the middle initial of Roger O. Thornhill stands for nothing) who gradually comes to care for someone enough to risk his life, Grant gives a performance of supreme polish and poise. As in his other Hitchcock performances, there is a dark side to his character – in Thornhill's case, selfishness, irresponsibility, a tendency to alcoholism – beneath the debonair facade. He was never better than in his films for Hitchcock, which is also true of James Stewart and Ingrid Bergman, and rather belies Hitchcock's insistence that he was more interested in the camera than in his characters.

"Actors are like cattle," Hitchcock would say, but the performances he conjured from them were anything but bovine or routine. All the performances of **North by Northwest** are impeccably judged. Eva Marie Saint, as the American agent, is the archetypal Hitchcock blonde, exuding a suspenseful sexuality that smolders tantalizingly before it ignites. James Mason, as Vandamm, is the most suave and insinuating of Hitchcock's many gentlemen villains, whilst Jessie Royce Landis is the most scattily insensitive of Hitchcock's mothers ("You boys aren't *really* trying to kill my son, are you?").

Prairie paranoia

Hitchcock's exploitation of the dramatic contrast between bizarre foreground and benign background has seldom been more ingeniously demonstrated than in **North by Northwest**. A hotel lobby is the setting for kidnapping, the United Nations building for murder, and the stone face of Mount Rushmore for perilous pursuit.

Most famously, Hitchcock even injects paranoia into a prairie setting, when Thornhill is sprayed with bullets from a crop-dusting biplane that has been "dusting crops where there ain't no crops". It is Hitchcock's most dazzling reversal of thriller cliché: here the dark deed takes place in bright sunlight. It is also a setpiece that is brilliantly set up by the film, establishing a hero who is the embodiment of urban man and then suddenly depositing him in a setting where he is small, vulnerable and exposed. And it shows his arrival at the scene from a vantage point that subtly implies danger without revealing precisely what it is. This crop-dusting episode is an object lesson in how to prepare and pace a suspense sequence.

American monument

Apart from the technique, what makes **North by Northwest** exceptional amongst comedy thrillers is the maturity of its relationships and the perceptive cynicism of its politics. The central love relationship has the kind of tensions one has observed elsewhere in Hitchcock.

As in **Vertigo**, the girl falls in love with the man almost out of guilt at setting him up; and as in **Suspicion** (1941) and **Spellbound** (1945) she makes love to a man who could be a murderer. For his part, he seems only too willing to be ensnared by a sexual siren who might be summoning him to his doom. His slick compliment to her at the station, "You're the smartest girl I ever spent a night with in a train," looks more dubious and cruel the more one thinks about it. The love scene itself is edgily filmed in the kind of

North by Northwest *(1959).*
▲ *Murder at the United Nations building in New York City. Cary Grant catches the dead body of a UN representative (Philip Ober) and instinctively clutches at the knife in his back, making it seem that he is the murderer.*

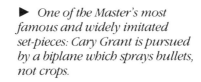

▶ *One of the Master's most famous and widely imitated set-pieces: Cary Grant is pursued by a biplane which sprays bullets, not crops.*

Overleaf: *The end of the murderous biplane. Cary Grant flags down a truck, the low-flying plane cannot avoid it and crashes into its side. Grant emerges unscathed from beneath the vehicle.*

▲ *Cary Grant gets himself out of a tight spot by behaving so outrageously at an art auction, in* **North by Northwest**, *that the police are sent for. They duly escort him from the building under the noses of the enemy agents who are trying to kill him.*

close, intimate camerawork one remembers from **Notorious** (1946), and the tense, antagonistic love triangle of **North by Northwest** is reminiscent of the earlier film.

Politically, the film also has a comment to make about the callous exploitation and abuse of individuals for minor political advantage in a deadly game of strategy, performance, bluff and double-bluff.

"War is hell, Mr Thornhill, even a cold one," says the Professor, to which Thornhill savagely replies: "If you fellows can't lick the Vandamms without asking girls like her to bed down with them and fly away with them and probably never come back alive, maybe you better start learning to *lose* a few cold wars."

But it would be unwise to distort the emphasis of the various elements. Lots of familiar Hitchcock ingredients are bubbling in **North by Northwest**: the theme of the wrong man, the pre-

cariousness of identity, the ineffectuality of the police. The ultimate effect, however, is of a dazzling and exhilarating cinematic display, the American Dream played out as potential nightmare but in broad daylight and to a resoundingly triumphant conclusion. Hitchcock might play irreverent games with American monuments in **North by Northwest** but its achievement is such that it has become something of an American monument itself.

Murderous monochrome

On the face of it, nothing could be more different from **North by Northwest** than the film which followed it, **Psycho**, the most famous, controversial and commercially successful of Hitchcock's entire career. From the high-spirited gallop across some of America's most spectacular sights and scenery in **North by North-**

▲ *After the excitement, at the end of* **North by Northwest***, advertising man Cary Grant and spy Eva Marie Saint marry and begin their honeymoon on a train. "The train entering the tunnel after the love scene between Grant and Saint is a phallic symbol,"* Hitchcock told the critics of Cahiers du Cinéma, *"only don't tell anyone!"*

Overleaf: *A mysterious figure stands guard by a Gothic house in which monstrous secrets lurk; Anthony Perkins in* **Psycho** *(1960).*

west, we move to an image of an America of forbidding gray anonymity – dingy offices and rooms, malevolent motels, seedy cellars. From the colorful expensive gloss of the earlier film, we move to a world of murderous monochrome.

Hitchcock used his television cameraman, John L. Russell, on **Psycho** rather than Robert Burks (who had worked consistently for him since **Strangers on a Train**) and when asked why **Psycho** was shot in black-and-white, Hitchcock had a simple reply: "Because of the blood."

However, there are two aspects of **North by Northwest** which **Psycho** shares. One is an obsession with identity (also a powerful theme of **Vertigo** and one that significantly recurs in **Marnie**). In **North by Northwest** the hero, having failed to convince his tormentors of his true identity, is finally persuaded by the Professor to impersonate someone who does not exist. In **Psycho**, the identity of the hero, Norman Bates (Anthony Perkins) is finally completely merged with that of his mother, who has been dead for ten years.

The second connection between the two films is a fear which infuses the crop-dusting episode of **North by Northwest**, and practically the whole length of **Psycho**: a fear of death suddenly striking out at you from nowhere. When Hitchcock was asked what appealed to him about **Psycho** and decided him to do the picture, he replied: "The suddenness of the murder in the shower, coming, as it were, out of the blue."

Extreme violence

The victim of this murder, Marion Crane (Janet Leigh), is a secretary who has absconded with some of her employer's money in order

Psycho *(1960).*
◀ *Janet Leigh uses some of her stolen money to trade in her car for a less conspicuous model. The cramped, bare setting of the ladies' room is one of a number of settings in the opening half of the film that suggest a world of bleak anonymity. The mirror reflection suggests a character already in two minds about what she is doing, torn by her conscience. Janet Leigh's superb performance was deservedly nominated for a Best Supporting Actress Oscar.*

▶ *The cinema's most famous scream, as Janet Leigh, cleansing herself of her sins and planning to return the money, is attacked in the shower. The furious montage which follows, accompanied by the screaming violins in Bernard Herrmann's extraordinary score, was one of the director's most carefully designed scenes. Although the murder scene lasts only forty-five seconds, it took a week to shoot.*

to be with her lover. Stopping for a night in a strange motel run by Norman Bates, she starts to take a shower and is suddenly attacked with a knife by a tall, dark figure whose face we cannot see.

Although the sequence lasts for only about forty seconds, it took Hitchcock a week to shoot because of the complexity of the montage. Little visual gore is seen, but an impression of extreme violence is conveyed through the savage rhythm of the editing and Bernard Herrmann's extraordinary music, whose shrieking violins seem simultaneously to evoke the heroine's screams and the slashing of the killer's knife.

The ordinariness of the shower setting makes the violence all the more terrifying, since it suddenly exploits all the aspects of danger in taking a shower one tries not to think about: instability, vulnerability, and confinement. It is perhaps Hitchcock's most remark-able example of finding the nightmarish in the normal.

Equally powerful is the murder of the private detective, Arbogast (Martin Balsam). He has been investigating Marion's disappearance and climbs the stairs of the Bates house to talk to Norman's mother. From a high angle we see a figure rushing out at Arbogast with a knife. The camera placement allows Hitchcock to conceal the identity of the murderer, but it also adds to the impact of the moment when Arbogast is attacked. Hitchcock jumps from the smallest image he could contrive to a huge close-up of Arbogast's shocked, bloody face.

"It was like music, you see," Hitchcock told Truffaut, "the high shot with the violins, and suddenly the big head with the brass instruments clashing."

Cruel, dead eyes

Psycho is a kind of symphony in two movements. The first movement is an unremittingly tense exposition, moving from normality to abnormality, light to dark, and culminating in Marion's murder and Norman's shout of "O God! Mother, mother! Blood, blood!"

Everything in the first forty minutes of the film is seen through the eyes of a frightened, disturbed heroine. This is what makes the film so taut and why her murder is so surprising and shocking. Her encounter with the traffic cop is particularly frightening. His dark glasses staring at her introduce the theme of "cruel" or "dead" eyes which is to run through the film. The encounter has little narrative purpose, but, symbolically, the policeman represents the surfacing of her guilty conscience.

The conscience theme is continued in an extraordinary car drive through the rain, in which Marion is tormented by voices in her head. Herrmann's pounding music seems possessed by the Furies, and the flashing lights appear to transform the vehicle into a kind of torture chamber. The purpose of all this is to get the heroine, and the audience, to that fateful motel in a specific frame of mind: frightened, vulnerable and off guard.

The second movement of the film, in which Marion's sister, Lila (Vera Miles), and her lover, Sam (John Gavin), discover the murderer, is a more relaxed set of variations. The characters of Lila and Sam seem less intense, more normalized mirror images of the tor-

Psycho *(1960).*
▲ *Anthony Perkins recoils in horror from the murdered body in* **Psycho**. *The film is full of bird imagery (note the picture on the wall) and anticipates* **The Birds** *(1963), Hitchcock's next film.*

▶ *The final scream, as Vera Miles comes to the end of her search for the secret of her sister's disappearance and stares into the limitless depths of depravity and decadence.*

mented figures of Marion and Norman. Hitchcock felt that, having planted the horror in the mind of the audience with the first murder, he could decrease the violence. The audience's imagination could now supply sufficient tension on its own, without too much prompting from him. There are two big shocks to come (the murder of the detective and the discovery of Mother in the cellar), but the film is less intense.

The scene with the sheriff, and the psychiatrist's explanation for Norman's transvestism and schizophrenia, that have turned him into a killer, are particularly labored. Nevertheless, Arbogast's cross-examination of Norman has the tense spontaneity of semi-improvisation and is brilliantly acted by Martin Balsam and Anthony Perkins. And the film's final images are tremendous. A womb-like image of a prison cell with Norman as a small figure in the center of the frame is followed by a brief internal monologue, in which Mother appears to be speaking to Norman from beyond the grave. Her grinning skull is briefly superimposed on Norman's face as if to suggest the final disintegration of his personality. Then Hitchcock dissolves to a shot of Marion's car being dragged from the swamp – dragged back into the light, as it were, but hideously covered in slime.

Major breakthrough

Although it had a mixed reception from the critics when it first appeared, **Psycho** is now universally accepted as a classic of the modern film. Its radical way with narrative, in which audience manipulation is much more important than character empathy, represented a major shift from the complacent conventions of plot-orientated popular cinema. Its grim portrait of family relationships and sexual abnormality influenced American horror movies for the next generation.

For all the excellence of the performances of Anthony Perkins, Janet Leigh and Martin Balsam, and Bernard Herrmann's spine-chilling score, the star of the show was undoubtedly Alfred Hitchcock himself. Everything in **Psycho** was ultimately dependent on his ghoulish genius, and the film's runaway success put him at the top of his profession. Unlike his characters, he seemed able to get away with anything.

▶ *Anthony Perkins in a tense pose that was used to publicize the film. Perkins knew that this role might be the biggest risk of his career and has expressed gratitude for the way Hitchcock directed the film, lightening the grisly plot with deft humor. He rewarded Hitchcock in turn with a performance of rare sensitivity and daring.*

One of the most striking features of **Psycho** is the recurrent bird imagery. Norman has stuffed birds hung up in his room, whose cruel eyes seem to follow his every move. In his very moving conversation with Marion, he says: "You know what I think? I think that we're all in our private traps . . . and none of us can ever get out. We scratch and claw, but only at the air, only at each other."

It is almost as if Hitchcock were subconsciously preparing for his next film, **The Birds**, in which, towards the end, the delirious heroine does literally try to scratch and claw at the air. Also, the characters have to erect their own cage to protect themselves from attack by birds, which have inexplicably declared war on the human race.

Enigmas

"I have a phrase to myself," said Hitchcock, "I always say that logic is dull." **The Birds** is not an illogical film. It is an anti-logic film, in which the attempt to explain away the bird attacks by people like the sheriff in the Brenner home and the ornithologist in the cafe delays the process of acting responsibly and even costs lives.

The narrative is full of enigmas. Why do the birds attack? What is the significance of the lovebirds, which Melanie Daniels (Tippi Hedren) has brought as a present for the kid sister of Mitch Brenner (Rod Taylor)? Is there a causal relationship between Melanie's arrival in Bodega Bay and the horror of what follows? By raising and refusing to answer these questions, Hitchcock ensures that the complacency of these characters has been completely undermined, which is one of the main themes of the film.

The Birds is Hitchcock's most technically innovative film. The electrical effects on the soundtrack are superbly orchestrated, and the four hundred trick shots involving the birds move Hitchcock's cinema into the realm of special effects. (When asked by a lady journalist how he had managed to make birds act so well, Hitchcock replied, politely: "They were very well paid, ma'am.")

In a way, **The Birds** is Hitchcock's closest film to Disney, a violent cartoon in which the fantasy creatures attack "real" people. It is also Hitchcock's most apocalyptic film, with an underlying exhoration to "Mend your ways, the end of the world may be nigh . . ."

Unlike the opening forty minutes of **Psycho**, which screws the film's tension to its highest point, the opening of **The Birds** has sometimes been criticized for being slow and languid. But the opening encounter in the bird shop between Melanie and Mitch, whose surface antagonism conceals immediate attraction, is full of little ironies. The basic situation is one that the film will later reverse, to show the humans in their gilded cages and the birds on the outside looking in.

▶ *Tippi Hedren makes her screen debut in the main role in* **The Birds** *(1963). She had been a leading fashion model whom Hitchcock had spotted on a breakfast-time television commercial. She was the last in Hitchcock's distinguished line of beautiful blondes whose cool exterior is gradually broken down by events.*

What follows is equally important. Melanie follows Mitch to Bodega Bay with a present of lovebirds which is really a sort of practical joke. She encounters Mitch's former girlfriend, Annie (Suzanne Pleshette), and his mother (Jessica Tandy) whose edgy exchanges with Melanie imply a hostility that their civilized exterior hypocritically suppresses.

Mitch and Melanie seem trapped in a game of surface and satirical sparring. The birds serve as an externalization of this inner tension. A story of lovebirds becomes a story of hatebirds, and what starts out as a peck on Melanie's head develops into a wholesale assault on her world. It is almost as if the birds come out of the sky in anger at human behavior, ripping apart the evasions, deceptions and snobbishness of these people and forcing them to discover a new sincerity and courage.

Territory of terror

Some scenes are as good as anything Hitchcock ever directed. A sequence in which Mitch and the sheriff argue about an invasion by sparrows of the Brenner home is visually dominated by the behavior of Mitch's mother, Mrs Brenner. Her slow clearing up of the broken china seems both an attempt to piece normality together and an indication of her own fragility in the face of the coming horror. The motif of china is continued in a following scene when Mrs Brenner visits a nearby farm and, prior to discovering the farmer's dead body, has a shiver of premonition on catching sight of a row of smashed cups hanging by their handles. When Melanie later brings her some tea, the shocked Mrs Brenner begins at last to open up (this is wonderfully acted by Jessica Tandy) and Melanie offers to collect Cathy, Mitch's young sister, from school.

Another classic scene follows. As Melanie waits for Cathy outside the school, the birds mass behind her in preparation for an attack on the children, turning the playground into a territory of terror.

The Birds *(1963)*.
◀ *The sky quickly blackens as crows attack a group of schoolchildren. The child in the center of the frame in the role of the hero's kid sister is Veronica Cartwright, later to become an equally accomplished adult actress in such films as* **Invasion of the Body Snatchers** *(1978)*, **Alien** *(1979) and* **The Right Stuff** *(1983)*.

▲ *Rod Taylor tries to stop a bird invading his home. This attack on the house was conveyed almost entirely by sound; the actors' movements conveying their terror were improvised spontaneously on set – an unusual practice for Hitchcock.*

The sly way Hitchcock builds the scene, by showing one bird, then four, then concealing his full hand until Melanie turns, surrounded, is suspense film craft of the highest class.

Not all of the special effects are equally convincing. There is one stunning bird's-eye-view shot of Bodega Bay as the birds mass for an imminent attack. And there's a tremendous scene where Melanie is trapped in a phone booth with birds milling outside, an exact reversal of her situation in the opening scene. On the other hand, the scene where sparrows invade the Brenner house earlier in the film is technically unconvincing. The wild arm-movements of the cast and the flight of the birds are clearly taking place on different strips of film.

Interestingly, the characters behave similarly when the birds attack the home at the end and when we only hear and do not see

The Birds (1963).

◄ *"Cover your faces, cover your eyes!" cries Rod Taylor (center) as sparrows burst down the chimney into the living room. Tippi Hedren (left) takes evasive action. At this stage the birds have not killed anyone, but the complacency of the community is being progressively undermined.*

▼ *As in nearly all the attacks we see, Tippi Hedren (here protecting herself) seems to be aware of the imminent danger a split second sooner than anyone else – as if there is some strange telepathy between her and the birds. "They say when you came, the whole thing started," a terrified housewife says to her. "I think you're the cause of all this – I think you're evil."*

them. (By this time, Hitchcock can convey terror through sound alone.) Their gestures again recall the words of Norman Bates about human beings "caught in private traps" and "clawing at the air and at each other".

Given the technical nature of the subject and indeed the film's own scathing attitude to humanity, one would not expect the actors to dominate. Rod Taylor and newcomer Tippi Hedren perform competently, and Suzanne Pleshette and Jessica Tandy play their scenes with great sensitivity, but again it is Hitchcock's triumph, demonstrating that he does not need stars and scarcely even needs characters in order to flay the emotions of his audience.

Disturbing portrait of courtship

After her debut in **The Birds** (and after Grace Kelly had declined Hitchcock's request to make a screen comeback in the leading role), Tippi Hedren was cast to play the title role in Hitchcock's **Marnie**. Beneath the beautiful and poised persona she presents to the world, Marnie is a compulsive thief and sexually frigid, with a mysterious terror of thunderstorms and the color red. Like the other heroines in this quintet of films, she is also a liar who is made to suffer disproportionately the consequences of her lying.

Her punishment is Mark Rutland (Sean Connery), an ex-zoologist and sexual blackmailer who threatens to turn Marnie over to the police if she does not agree to marry him. Sean Connery's brilliant performance as Rutland masterfully exudes a cruel, wary fascination for the heroine that steadily builds into one of the most disturbing portraits of courtship and desire in Hitchcock's entire output. His liberation of Marnie from her mental trauma is the substance of the drama but one cannot help feeling that, with Rutland as her predatory mate, Marnie's problems might conceivably be just beginning.

Marnie (1964).
◀ *Tippi Hedren in the title role of the first "woman's picture" Hitchcock had made for a long time and one of his most controversial and audacious psychological melodramas. Here Marnie is checking the combination of the safe before carrying out the robbery.*

▶ *Marital rape. The husband (Sean Connery) has discovered Marnie's frigidity on their nightmare honeymoon cruise and has agreed not to touch her. But now his sexual frustration overcomes him and he tears at her clothes, the nightdress falling to her feet. Hitchcock, as usual, implies nudity instead of showing it directly, achieving much more powerful results.*

Marnie *(1964).*
▼   *Tippi Hedren and Sean
Connery. Marnie's riding gear is a
reminder of her love of horses,
which is a temporary release from
her inner tensions and an
oppressive male world. To Mark
(Connery), Marnie is a
fascinating wild animal whom he
must first corner and then tame.*

Strange and haunting

Marnie is one of the strangest and most haunting of Hitchcock's movies. Rutland's world of business, horses and such English pursuits as fox-hunting and afternoon tea reminds one of the heroine's family in **Suspicion**. It also contrasts strikingly with Marnie's background of the repression and religious fanaticism of the American South. One of the continual fascinations of the film is that each of the main characters (Marnie, Mark, Marnie's mother, Mark's sister-in-law, even Mark's business associate Strutt) has his or her own eccentric morality that conflicts violently with everyone else's: decency against deviousness, dependence on the past against freedom from the past.

Equally, the style of the film seems to move freely between simulated reality and blatant artificiality. The intricate and compelling sexual conflict between Mark and Marnie has a realism that sometimes clashes with the film's obvious back-projection and a stylized street set for Marnie's home that has a painted backdrop of a harbor at the end of the street. This is an early clue to the root of Marnie's trauma about red and storms: the fact that, as a child, on a stormy night, she had bloodily killed a sailor who was struggling with her hysterical mother, then a prostitute.

The sheer obviousness of these devices appalled many critics and aroused some derision from audiences. Yet this balance between reality and abstraction was already part of Hitchcock's stylistic apparatus in **The Birds**, and **Marnie** is actually about the collision between the real world and dream worlds that both Marnie and her husband have erected.

Fetish or love

Hitchcock has analyzed disordered personalities before. What is unique about **Marnie** is that he gives us two for the price of one. Marnie's hang-ups, which include displacing her distaste for men with a love of horses, derive from a tormented childhood, a deprivation of maternal love, and an oppressive insistence on "decency" that has led to deceit and sexual repression. In this respect, **Marnie** is a moving study of a single woman trying confusedly to operate in a world of men and still somehow maintain both her sexual and her financial independence.

If anything, Rutland seems more disturbed than she is, for his sexual attraction for Marnie seems more in the nature of a fetish than love. For him, his courtship of Marnie is almost an extension of his zoological pursuits. She is a wild animal whom he has tracked and cornered and whom he must now tame. He starts reading books on the criminality of the female as if Marnie is not simply his wife but an interesting case study. The question is: once the subject has been mastered, will Rutland lose interest?

The suspense of the film is relatively low key. A wordless robbery scene is immaculately shot and very tense, Hitchcock using a filing cabinet to divide the film frame into two and show Marnie's robbery of the safe on one side of the screen and a cleaner entering to mop up the office on the other.

More characteristic, however, is the suspense generated by the wary interaction of character. Mark's unpeeling of Marnie's mask during a long car drive (car drives are very important in all these five films). Marnie's first interview at Rutland's, where the camera tells a story (Mark's dawning suspicions of her) that is quite different from the story the dialogue is telling (Marnie's qualifications for the job). Here we have the essence of Hitchcock cinema.

Equally good is a strange encounter at a racetrack with a sinister man who claims to know Marnie. It has no more plot purpose than the scene with the cop in **Psycho**, but it implies the kind of sleazy situations and individuals Marnie has eluded in the past but which might have awaited her in the future without Mark's intervention. As he tells her, some *other* sexual blackmailer might have trapped her and not been so sympathetic.

Marnie has its dull and dubious moments, but it is finely acted by the whole cast. Diane Baker as Mark's jealous sister-in-law, Lil, Louise Latham as Marnie's mother, and Martin Gabel as Strutt are as impressive as the principals. And this time Bernard Herrmann's surging score is richly romantic. It might not be the finest of this stunning quintet of films, but it serves as a summation of Hitchcock's work at this time: the bold and unusual technique, the increasingly complex probings into areas of human sexuality and individual identity, not to mention subsidiary themes to do with female criminality, male carnality, and maternal possessiveness.

Cry of anguish

For all of Hitchcock's habitual deflection of questions relating to the themes and personal preoccupations of his movies, there is a real cry of anguish lurking within them.

"Why don't you love me, mother? I always wondered why you didn't," says Marnie. "If you love someone, you don't do that to them, even if you hate them," says Norman Bates in **Psycho**, angrily resisting Marion's suggestion that his mother might be better off in an institution. The difficulty of love is an obsessive theme in these movies.

As a final thought, consider the lovebirds in **The Birds**, and that moment when they lean to one side or the other when Melanie swerves the car on her way to Bodega Bay. It is a joke and makes them seem endearing but it is also investing them with a sort of human characteristic and intelligence that will mark the behavior of the hatebirds.

The lovebirds are innocent and survive, but their coloring is green and red like the flesh and clothes of Melanie, who is accused of starting the whole horror. They are an optimistic symbol, but when they first arrive and Mrs Brenner and Annie, the schoolteacher, learn what they are, they both react in the same tense way: "Oh, I see," as if these birds are somehow part of the emotional threat that Melanie represents.

When Hitchcock was asked about that, he made a comment that might serve as a summary of what these five unnervingly brilliant movies are basically about: "It all goes to show that with a little effort, even the word 'love' can be made to sound ominous."

Overleaf: *The robbery. Tippi Hedren (right) has just become aware of the cleaner in the adjoining part of the office and is about to remove her shoes so she can steal away quietly. The arrival of the cleaner on the left side of the screen while Marnie was emptying the safe on the right side was shown in a single, detached, long shot, which Hitchcock thought less conventional and more suspenseful than cutting between the two planes of action.*

Although they have their moments of panache, passion and power, Hitchcock's last four films – **Torn Curtain** (1966), **Topaz** (1969), **Frenzy** (1972) and **Family Plot** (1976) – represent a definite decline in achievement. Nevertheless, it would have been unreasonable to expect him to sustain the excellence of his 1958-64 output. Also, the reasons for the decline are quite intricate and involved.

Team spirit

Unquestionably one of the factors that had contributed to the brilli-ance of Hitchcock's work during the previous decade was his assembly of a team of expert technicians on whom he could rely to realize, even enhance, his intentions. Notably, these included the editor George Tomasini, cameraman Robert Burks and composer Bernard Herrmann. None of them worked on his final films.

◄ *Anna Massey plays another of the necktie murderer's victims in* **Frenzy** *(1972). Later the murderer realizes that she has grasped his distinctive diamond tie-pin in the struggle, and that he must return to the truck in which he has dumped her body to retrieve it.*

▲ *The fight at the farmhouse in* **Torn Curtain** *(1966), in which the American scientist (Paul Newman, left) comes to grips with an East German security agent (Wolfgang Kieling), who has discovered the real purpose of Newman's mission. The agent has to be killed without anyone's hearing. The ensuing murder by knife, spade and finally gas oven is one of the most gruesome in Hitchcock's work.*

Torn Curtain *(1966).*

◄ *Paul Newman is greeted at the airport by newsmen who wish to hear about the defection to East Germany of this important American scientist. Newman is watched by fiancée Julie Andrews, who has known nothing of his plans and she, in turn, is watched by Günter Strack, part of the East German delegation supervising Newman's defection. Like Claude Rains in* **Notorious**, *Strack is distracted from his political responsibilities by romantic infatuation.*

▼ *Hitchcock directing Newman for the scene in which he emerges from the plane.*

► *Newman has created havoc by shouting "Fire!" at the theater and, in the ensuing confusion, tries to escape with his fiancée from the East German authorities. Julie Andrews (center frame) is struggling towards the exit while the East German security chief (Hans-Jörg Felmy, top left) is trying to capture her.*

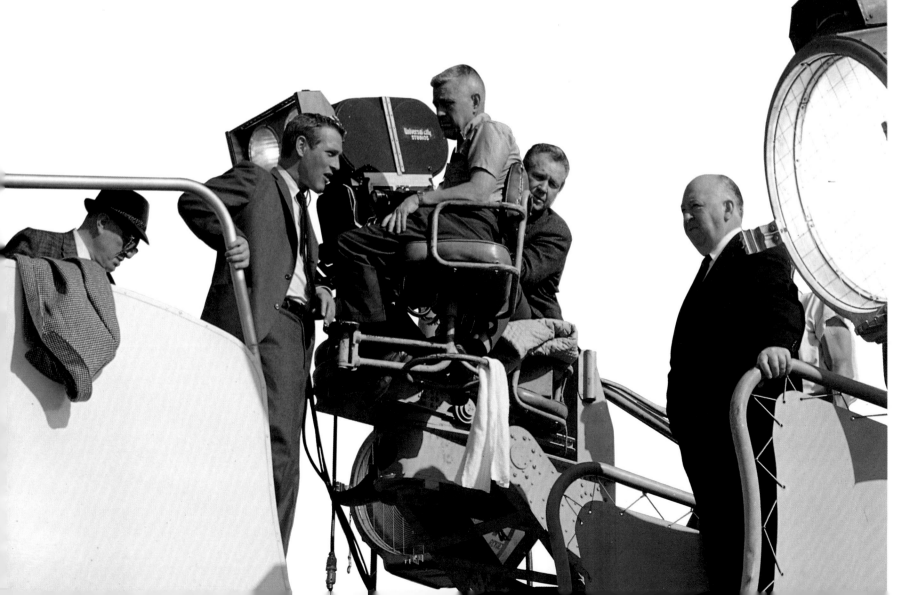

Tomasini died in 1964 while working on Otto Preminger's **In Harm's Way** (1965). None of Hitchcock's final quartet of films had the razor-sharp editing that Tomasini characteristically provided: **Topaz**, in particular, is woefully slack.

Robert Burks died in 1968, and again, none of Hitchcock's later films had the crisp quality Burks had provided almost consistently since **Strangers on a Train** (1951). The camerawork on **Torn Curtain** and **Frenzy** is no more than competent. On **Topaz** and **Family Plot** it is sometimes even less than that.

The most significant loss, though, was that occasioned by the break-up between Hitchcock and composer Bernard Herrmann. Herrmann's scores for Hitchcock are undoubtedly some of the finest ever written for motion pictures, and this composer/director partnership was at least as significant as that between Prokofiev and Sergei Eisenstein or William Walton and Laurence Olivier. The neurotic romanticism of **Vertigo** (1958) and the tingling suspense of **Psycho** (1960) are almost inconceivable without Herrmann's musical contributions.

The argument that severed their relationship was over Herrmann's music for **Torn Curtain**. Apparently, Hitchcock had wanted a more popular, tuneful score, reflecting the tastes of the times but also reflecting the relatively uncomplicated melodrama of the film. Instead, Herrmann's score consisted of bleak sound blocks of grayness and iron. His music was thrown out, and the partnership dissolved, Hitchcock replacing him on the film with John Addison's less imaginative talents. Herrmann thought Hitchcock had sold out, although the appropriateness or otherwise of Herrmann's brutal music for the film can now be assessed. There is a gramophone recording of that music conducted by Elmer Bernstein (an almost unprecedented example of a film soundtrack recording of a score that was never used).

Indisputably, however, none of the scores for Hitchcock's future films came anywhere near the quality of Herrmann's work. Interestingly, Hitchcock was to have a very similar disagreement with Henry Mancini over the latter's savage score for **Frenzy**, replacing it with one in much lighter vein from Ron Goodwin.

Increasingly insecure

Perhaps the occasional tensions between Hitchcock and his collaborators in this final phase are symptomatic of a more general feeling of unease in the maestro. In the 1950s and early 1960s, Hitchcock seemed in tune with the industry and with the audience. For various reasons, particularly after the critical and commercial failure of **Marnie**, this partnership seemed increasingly insecure.

The advertising campaigns for the films seemed to have less flair and confidence than for **Psycho** and **The Birds** (1963). After the failure of **Torn Curtain**, the casts of the films became less auspicious, and none of the last three films has any obvious identification figure. Hitchcock is now the main star, but the master chef is preparing his dishes for a younger audience that has markedly different appetites from the audiences of old.

Part of the appeal of Hitchcock in the heyday of his popularity had been what he could get away with. As he had said in 1937: "The art of directing for the commercial market is to know just how far you can go . . . I hope in time to have more freedom still – if audiences give it to me." For thirty years, Hitchcock's capacity to shock, either with moments that were sexier than the norm or more violent than is usually tolerated in popular cinema, had seemed limitless. But what happens in a permissive cinema when the restraints on sex and violence are lifted? Hitchcock's former daring becomes the convention and the impact considerably decreased.

Faced with that situation, a director like Hitchcock has only two choices. He can attempt to go further in outrageousness, or he can mellow by refining familiar themes. Part of the failure of the last four films comes from Hitchcock's indecision about which course he should follow.

On the one hand, he goes further in that the murder scenes of **Torn Curtain** and **Frenzy** are graphic, extended and terrifying. They are also dangerously close to being actively distasteful, for they disrupt the relatively oldfashioned context in which they are placed. On the other hand, the films are either dismayingly or disarmingly out-of-date. **Torn Curtain** and **Topaz** return us to the world of political espionage that Hitchcock had explored in the 1940s. **Frenzy** is a funny and ferocious farewell to Hitchcock's British period. **Family Plot** is a light, airy comedy-thriller with twinges of death and mortality.

Clash of stars

In **Torn Curtain** an American scientist (Paul Newman) defects to Eastern Europe, followed by his reluctant fiancée (Julie Andrews). It is no surprise to learn that the defection is not genuine, and that his real mission is to steal a secret mathematical formula from a professor in Leipzig.

As the girl who disapproves of her fiancé's defection and only slowly learns of his real mission, Julie Andrews has to play a character several steps slower than the average audience and the strain shows. Newman's uneasy performance reflects the antagonistic relationship that grew between him and Hitchcock, the latter finding Newman's analytical acting methods (like Montgomery Clift's in **I Confess**, 1953) in conflict with his style of directing actors. Hitchcock always built his performances through looks and montage. He did not relish intense discussion of psychological motivation.

The suspense sequences have a certain panache: the mathematical cat-and-mouse game on the blackboard between the American and East German scientists, each attempting to probe what the other knows; an exciting chase scene on a bus hired to help Newman and Andrews escape; a riot in a theater precipitated by Newman's sudden shout of "Fire!" when he is in imminent danger of arrest.

Most disturbing is the murder scene at the farmhouse, when an East German official discovers the real reason for the American's defection and has to be silenced. Spade, knife and gas oven are needed before the victim's frantic struggles for life are finally overpowered. Explaining the reasons for the incongruous gruesomeness of the scene, Hitchcock insisted: "I wanted to show how difficult it is to kill a man." He showed instead his difficulty in gauging the tastes of modern audiences.

Curious and uncertain

Torn Curtain is a curious and uncertain film. After **Marnie** had revisited the themes of **Spellbound** (1945) with superior results, **Torn Curtain** seems an attempt to rework **Notorious** (1946) for the 1960s. Although it has nothing like the character complexity and narrative grip of the earlier film, it has something of its uncomfortable tone.

The hero is less of a patriot than a plagiarist, and one could take **Torn Curtain** as a Faustian tale about a scientist who sells his integrity for ultimate knowledge and, in so doing, consigns his soul to damnation. Hence the credit title design of faces grimacing in a haze of smoke and cloud. Hence the American's presence at and disruption of a ballet performance of *Francesca da Rimini*, Tchaikovsky's musical tone-poem inspired by an episode from Dante's *Inferno* and in which the souls of two lovers are swept into the flames of hellfire.

The hero's selfish behavior endangers the lives of many finer people who work to help him, and a political interpretation of the film as an allegory of America's blundering global interference (at the time of Vietnam) is not entirely invalid. However, a serious political statement would need a much more persuasive dramatic structure than **Torn Curtain** provides.

▲ *Paul Newman and Julie Andrews at the Stockholm quayside in* **Torn Curtain**, *having jumped to safety from a ship taking them to freedom from East Germany.*

That political cinema is not Hitchcock's forte was conclusively demonstrated in his following film, **Topaz**, quite the dreariest picture the Master ever made. This time the defection is from East to West and by a KGB official. His revelations about a secret arms deal between Cuba and the Soviet Union and about an organization of French officials in high office (codename Topaz), who are actually Soviet agents, cause consternation in American diplomatic circles. A diplomat from the French Embassy, André Devereaux (Frederick Stafford), is sent to investigate. It is Hitchcock's version of the Cuban Missile Crisis of 1962.

▼ *Hitchcock prepares an airfield shot in* **Topaz** *(1969), while staff, crew members and military personnel await his signal. The leading actor, Frederick Stafford, is on the extreme left; script supervisor Trudy von Trotha sits on the director's right; Hitchcock is discussing details with his production manager and associate for many years, Herbert Coleman.*

Perversely, to carry a story almost wholly devoid of dramatic incident, Hitchcock chose his dullest cast. The only remotely interesting performance is Philippe Noiret's as the second-in-command of the French traitors, and he does not appear until two-thirds of the way through the film. The principals are complete ciphers. It is as if Hitchcock saw the characters merely as impersonal counters in a game of detached but deadly international politics. But the ingredients are maladroitly mixed. The gadgetry and gaudiness of James Bond (sexy available women, cameras improbably hidden in ham rolls, and so forth) alternate with darker scenes of Cuban torture and all-round treachery.

The film's political balance is thrown by the crude caricaturing of the Cuban rebels, and one can imagine the conservative and anti-communist rhetoric of **Topaz** might have offended many young

Topaz (1969).
▼ *André (Frederick Stafford back to camera) and his daughter (Claude Jade, right) discover the body of Jarre (Philippe Noiret), one of the Frenchmen who heads* Topaz, *a Communist spy group that is located within the heart of French security.*

▶ *Two members of the pro-American, anti-Communist resistance network who are tortured by the Cuban authorities when their surveillance cameras are found. The woman is Carolyn Conwell, who also played the farmer's wife in* **Torn Curtain** *(1966).*

2026-10

Topaz *(1969).*

◄ *Hitchcock could not decide on a satisfactory ending for the film – this version was dropped after an unsuccessful preview. The Russian sympathizer (Michel Piccoli), challenged to a duel by the hero, has been assassinated by a sniper in a deserted stadium. In the final film, a shot of the entrance to Piccoli's Paris home is followed by a gunshot, indicating his suicide.*

▼ *A production shot with Tina Hedstrom (left) in the role of the Russian defector's daughter and John Forsythe (right) as an American intelligence agent. (Hitchcock had a macabre interest in dummies. Here Hedstrom is carrying one of herself.)*

2026

filmgoers in 1969. However, it is not so much the attitudes themselves that offend as their banality of expression. The Russian defector and his family are driven past the White House, at which point the daughter looks across at the building and comments banally and dutifully: "It's nice."

Deadly embrace

There is one fine scene. A Cuban general (John Vernon) has discovered that the widow (Karin Dor) of a hero of the Revolution has betrayed state secrets to Devereaux. To spare her from being tortured, he shoots her. Hitchcock directs the scene with intense intimacy. The camera circles the two in a deadly embrace that recalls the staging of the love scenes in **Notorious** and **North by Northwest** (1959). Suddenly a gunshot rings out, at which point Hitchcock cuts to an overhead shot of the heroine as she sinks to the floor, her purple dress spreading out beneath her like a soft carpet as she falls. Truffaut once said that one of Hitchcock's gifts was the ability to direct love scenes as if they were murder scenes, and vice-versa. This scene in **Topaz** is one of the clearest examples of what he meant. It has a disturbing beauty and a peculiar mixture of tenderness and terror. It almost redeems what is an otherwise wretched movie.

Black comedy in England

After the debacle of **Topaz**, Hitchcock's penultimate film, **Frenzy** (1972), seems almost a return to form. It was made in England and has something of the flavor of Hitchcock's earlier British films. A series of bizarre murders (women first raped then strangled with a necktie) all seem to point to a volatile ex-squadron leader (Jon Finch) as the likely perpetrator. The actual killer, however, is an outwardly charming Covent Garden fruit-merchant (Barry Foster). It is a typical Hitchcock story of the pursuit of two men, one of whom is innocent, the other guilty, the former increasingly trapped by circumstantial evidence, the latter leading a charmed life.

Frenzy *(1972).*
◄ *Bob Rusk (Barry Foster), a fruit merchant who is as nutty as a fruit cake, throws out a girl who does not share his sado-masochistic tastes. His apartment, above a respectable publishing company, is conveniently close to his work in London's Covent Garden.*

▶ *A macabre production still as Hitchcock seems to float abstractedly in the River Thames. This dummy was going to be used in the film but in the end only appeared in the promotional trailers.*

On one level, the film is a black comedy. It opens with a travelogue view over London, accompanied by a sub-Elgarian main theme by Ron Goodwin. A public speaker assures a crowd that "all the water will soon be clear . . . of the waste products of the society." His words are instantly undercut when the naked body of a murdered woman is spotted floating in the supposedly unpolluted river. This kind of joke is carried right the way through the film, Hitchcock offering a sly contrast between the quaint touristy facade of modern London and the polluted and ferocious undercurrent which reveals a capital city that is going to seed. There are quite a lot of jokes about diluted drinks and smelly food, as if London is both sinking and going putrid.

The black humor is extended into domestic scenes and murder scenes, each to do with troublesome food. The police inspector (Alec McCowen) discusses unappetizing details of the murder case over equally unappetizing "exotic" dinners prepared by his gourmet wife (Vivien Merchant), and somehow has to dispose of the appalling meals without his wife noticing. Similarly, the murderer is trapped in the back of a truck with one of his victims, whose body he has tried to hide in a sack of potatoes. Gruesomely he has to break the victim's fingers to retrieve his own distinctive tie-pin, which has come off in their life-and-death struggle. However, the potato dust will incriminate him, as will the unforeseen moment when the body falls out of the vehicle. Both scenes are lugubriously funny essays on the difficulty of disposing efficiently of dead matter.

Electrifying moments

Hitchcock dashes off a number of good surprises, notably two electrifying moments. The first is when the sound suddenly and ominously dips as an unsuspecting female is approached by the murderer. The second when the camera tracks slowly, silkily away from the door of the murderer's flat, down the stairs and into the street, and we stare across at a window behind which murder is being enacted.

Given some rather awkward, outdated dialogue by Anthony Shaffer, the performers all cope well. The women are well cast for their realism rather than their glamor. Barbara Leigh-Hunt's performance as Jon Finch's estranged wife is especially fine. Because of the tremulous terror she communicates when raped and then murdered, the scene becomes almost too horrible, more so than the shower murder in **Psycho**. It is some time before **Frenzy** recovers its lightly sardonic tone, which might very well have been Hitchcock's intention.

The disturbing quality of the scene (the victim reciting a consolatory psalm in eerie counterpoint to the killer's heavy breathing after the rape) comes from the uncomfortable combination of horror and excitement communicated by the filming. Because of this scene, the inspector's later comment that "religious and sexual mania are closely linked" seems almost applicable to Hitchcock himself. It is not surprising that his films have never endeared themselves to feminists.

The film's ferocity is sometimes excessive and unnerving but it is also commendably uncompromised. In a sense, **Frenzy** dares to go further than the more highly praised earlier film, **Strangers on a Train** (1951), with which it has a good deal in common. The plot is similar, with a culpable hero, a charming villain, and a scene which involves the strangulation by the killer of the hero's estranged wife. Yet **Frenzy** carries through its themes with a more

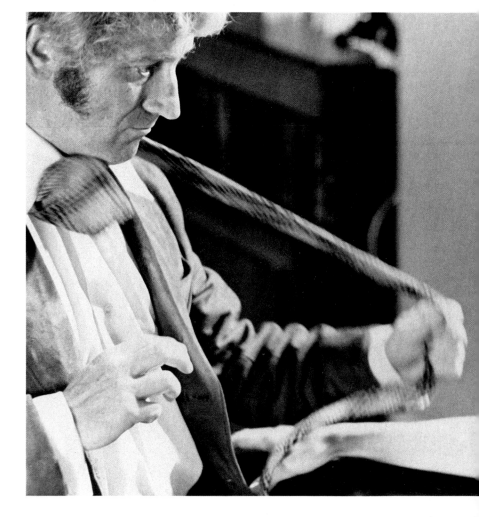

Frenzy (1972).
▲ *The horrific rape/murder scene as necktie murderer Barry Foster prepares to strangle the terrified Barbara Leigh-Hunt. A respectable, possibly repressed woman is suddenly trapped in her worst nightmare.*

▶ *The body of Barbara Leigh-Hunt after the murder. The gold cross on a chain around her neck is unable to resist the stronger pressure of the murderous necktie. After the rape, she grasps the crucifix on her neck and whispers a consoling psalm, almost as if to cast out evil spirits.*

ruthless logic. When Farley Granger ascended those stairs in **Strangers** to commit 'his' murder of Bruno's father, we never did believe he would go through with it, which in turn undermined the whole "Double" theme. But when Jon Finch ascends the stairs in **Frenzy** towards the end to avenge himself on Foster, we are not only convinced he will commit his murder: he actually does, but strikes out at the wrong target. He may not finally be the murderer, but the progress of the plot clearly reveals him to be capable of murder.

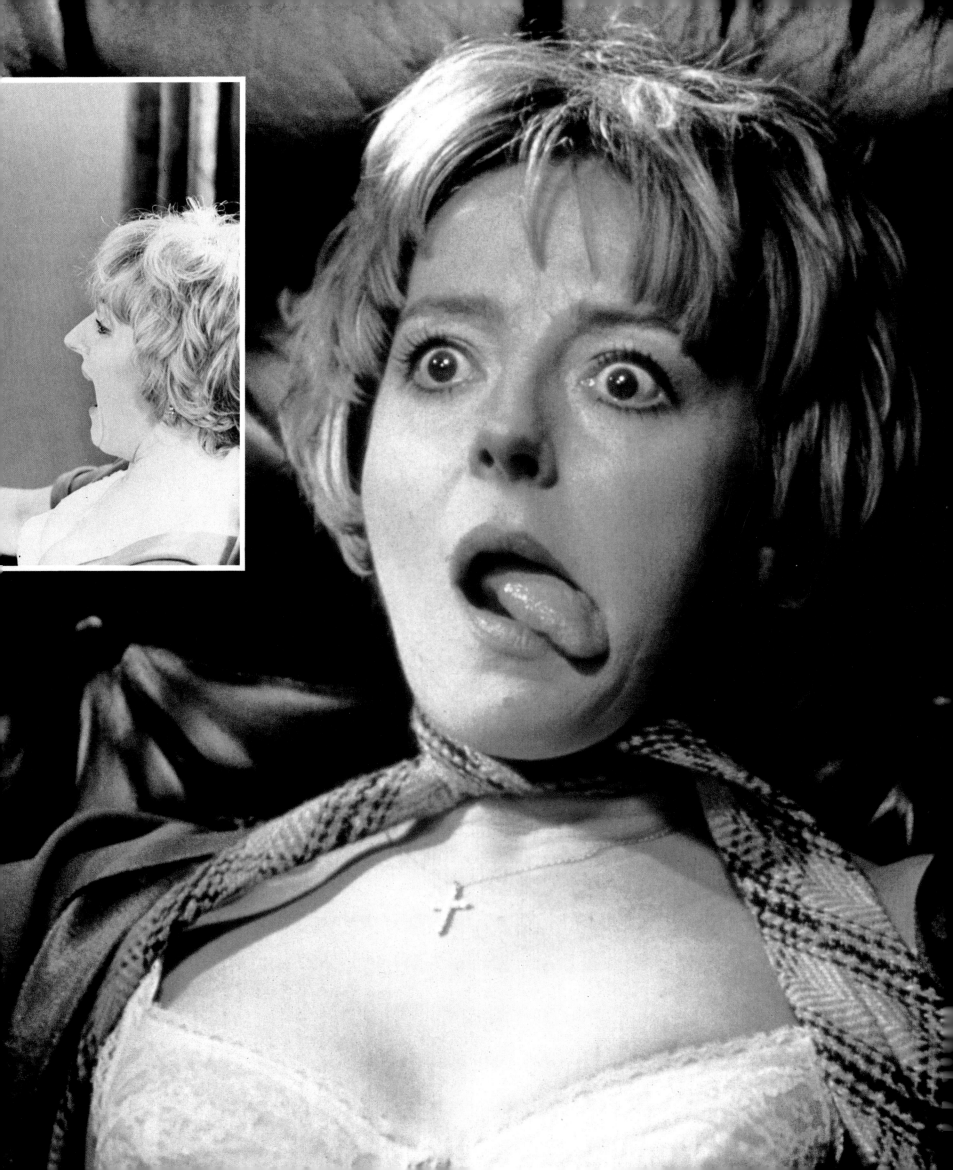

Swan song

Hitchcock's last film, **Family Plot**, is much more genial than **Frenzy**, but also slacker and less interesting. Based on Victor Canning's novel, *The Rainbird Pattern*, it reunited Hitchcock with his **North by Northwest** scenarist, Ernest Lehman, and is undoubtedly the best written of his last films. The involved plot, about a missing heir who turns out to be a jewel thief (William Devane) and who is sought by a taxi driver (Bruce Dern) and his psychic girlfriend (Barbara Harris) for the reward, affords Hitchcock a relaxed opportunity for a droll reprise of familiar themes.

Fittingly the tensest scenes (the kidnapping of a bishop; the scene where the hero's car goes out of control) are also the funniest. **Family Plot** is a reminder that the cinema's master of suspense was also a joker of genius. The double-plot structure springs a few surprises, when seemingly disconnected twin narratives suddenly collide. What makes the film seem rather lethargic are not so much faults as indulgences. There is an exposition scene that is stronger on atmosphere than pace; a performance by Barbara Harris that is kookier than the plot strictly requires; and a funereal visual humor (headstones that will not stay in the ground, gravediggers popping up out of nowhere) that seems excessive even for this family plot.

Hitchcock's own personal appearance in the film is in familiar silhouette behind the doors of an office marked: Registry of Births and Deaths. Although he was to prepare the script for another film, **The Short Night**, it was as if he sensed that **Family Plot** was his swan song. **The Trouble With Hitchcock**, one might have called it, and the expansive, relaxed style is like a slow exhalation. It was a modest, stylish, cheerful way to end: not with a bang, but with a wink at the audience.

Family Plot (1976).
▼ *Disguised in a blond wig, the missing nephew's accomplice (Karen Black) examines the diamond ransom for the kidnapped shipping magnate. After the opening sequence involving the medium and the old lady and the following conversation between the medium and her taxi-driver boyfriend, Karen Black's unexplained appearance seems to have dragged the film into a wholly unexpected direction. However, the apparently separate plots gradually inch their way together.*

▲ The medium, Barbara Harris (right), confers with wealthy Mrs Rainbird (Cathleen Nesbitt) over a bottle of sherry in the old lady's cluttered sitting room. Mrs Rainbird is hoping to trace her long-lost illegitimate nephew and offers a $10,000 reward.

◄ After surviving one attempt to kill them by tampering with the brakes of their own automobile, Bruce Dern and Barbara Harris now have to run for cover from Ed Lauter's maliciously aimed car. This exciting scene from **Family Plot**, like the famous crop-dusting episode in **North by Northwest**, gains a lot of suspense, humor and irony from its use of contrast and reversal of convention – the outrageous deed committed in broad daylight.

Family Plot *(1976)*.
▲ *The most famous suspense set-piece in the film: Bruce Dern (right) at the wheel of his car as it accelerates out of control; Barbara Harris (left) cringes in fear and clutches at his shoulder, interfering with Dern's attempt to control both the car and her.*

◄ *On the trail of the missing heir to a fortune, Bruce Dern begins to uncover even more mysteries. Here he is beginning to suspect that the young man, known as Edward Shoebridge, supposedly killed in a fire, is not really dead.*

144

REGISTRAR OF
BIRTHS & DEATHS

CONCLUSION:
INFLUENCE AND ACHIEVEMENT

▲ *Anthony Perkins re-creates his classic performance as Norman Bates in* **Psycho II** *(1983). The sequel had enough good ideas, surprises and originality to ensure another episode of the saga,* **Psycho III**, *which Perkins will direct himself.*

hough he died in 1980, Alfred Hitchcock is still the most famous and most imitated film director in the world. His impact on all aspects of modern cinema has been profound.

French admirers

The admiration of French film critics who, as directors, were to form the nucleus of the *nouvelle vague*, has already been mentioned. The films of François Truffaut and Claude Chabrol, in particular, are full of Hitchcock touches. What is interesting is the different side of Hitchcock to which they respond.

In films like **Fahrenheit 451** (1966) and **The Bride Wore Black** (1968), Truffaut imitated some of Hitchcock's suspense techniques (subjective camerawork, the rich deployment of moody Bernard Herrmann scores). Truffaut also responded to the romantic side of Hitchcock. **The Story of Adèle H.** (1975), with its heroine reduced to rags and madness by romantic disappointment, and **The Green Room** (1978), with its morbid hero intent on preserving the image of a loved one who has died, both owe an enormous amount to **Vertigo** (1958) in their presentation of analogous themes of romantic obsession.

Chabrol responds to the more demonic side of Hitchcock, exposing in a mocking tone the murderousness of family life and the hollowness of bourgeois values. Like Hitchcock, Chabrol's *métier* is the thriller. The best of his films, like **Les Bonnes Femmes** (1960) and **Le Boucher** (1970), slowly unpeel the layers of charm from their heroes to reveal the beast within, like Hitchcock's Uncle Charlie in **Shadow of a Doubt** (1943).

Young America

Hitchcock's influence has been equally pronounced on a younger generation of Hollywood directors, though at a more superficial level. Jonathan Demme's thriller **Last Embrace** (1979) is a parade of sub-Hitchcockian set-pieces – eventful train journeys, menacing moments in bell towers, falls from a height. In a rather more stylish way, so too is Robert Benton's **Still of the Night** (1982), which features Mcryl Strccp as thc mysterious blonde and includes more Hitchcock allusions than any film ever made.

A sequel to **Psycho** (1960), Richard Franklin's **Psycho II** (1983) draws inventively on Hitchcock's original imagery while, in **High Anxiety** (1977), Mel Brooks does his Hitchcockian homage by playing the head of a psychoneurotic Institute for the Very, Very Nervous who at one stage is splattered by birds.

Steven Spielberg's early movies, particularly **Duel** (1971) and **Jaws** (1975), draw heavily on the Hitchcock suspense style.

The work of Brian De Palma can hardly be understood without reference to its Hitchcock counterparts. **Obsession** (1976) is a virtual remake of **Vertigo. Carrie** (1976) alludes extensively to **Marnie**. Both **Sisters** (1973) and **Dressed to Kill** (1980) quote incessantly from **Psycho**.

In Britain, the richness of Nicolas Roeg's work derives partly from his absorption of crucial stylistic and thematic concerns of Hitchcock – the romanticism, the violence, the relation between cinema and voyeurism. Roeg's **Don't Look Now** (1973) is the greatest modern film thriller since Hitchcock in his prime, and **Bad Timing** (1980) is the commercial cinema's boldest study of voyeurism, necrophilism and romantic perversity since **Vertigo**.

▶ *Roy Scheider (left) in* **Last Embrace** *(1979), playing a paranoid investigator who really is being persecuted. Miklos Rozsa's heady music contributes to the* **Spellbound** *atmosphere.*

Uniquely fascinating

This is a selective rather than exhaustive list, but the question it raises is obvious. What is it about Hitchcock that has proved so uniquely fascinating to film makers, film theorists and film audiences alike? I suspect that film-makers have tended instinctively to consult Hitchcock's films not for their themes but for their technique.

Hitchcock had two priceless gifts for a film-maker which may sound commonplace but are actually the rarest qualities in a film director: the ability to tell a story through the camera; and the ability to make audiences the world over *emote*. Hitchcock always insisted that what universally stirred audiences about **Psycho** was not the message, nor the performances, nor the narrative, but the arousal of their emotions by "pure film". Of all modern directors, Spielberg is probably the one who has most closely followed that precept – the capacity of the film medium to induce mass emotion.

▲ *Guilty heroine Janet Margolin (left) embraces unbalanced investigator Roy Scheider (right) in Jonathan Demme's* **Last Embrace** *(1979), a racy homage to Hitchcock complete with falls from heights, suspense in a bell-tower, and a tone of dark romanticism.*

True individual

Hitchcock's own celebrity as a director must also account for some of the interest he has attracted, because it has wide implications. He showed that films could be sold on a director's name, and audiences would recognize and rely on that name as a guide to the kind of film they could expect. Hitchcock sometimes commented somewhat ruefully on this ("If I made 'Cinderella', they'd be looking for the body in the coach"). But the sensational achievements of **Psycho** and **The Birds** (1963) would have been unthinkable without that pre-existent relationship between famous director and intrigued audience.

He is the only director whose films constitute a genre in themselves, like the Western, or the gangster movie, or the musical. This permitted Hitchcock both to follow conventions he had initiated yet also to confound expectations by working clever and unpredictable variations. In that sense, Hitchcock's fame did enhance his artistry. In striving to keep one step ahead of his audience and yet keep his followers interested and guessing, he drove himself to more and more inventive inspirations. In the process, he showed it was possible for an individual to express himself creatively even in a commercial, industrial pleasure factory like Hollywood.

The arguments about Hitchcock as an artist, or *auteur*, have fluctuated and changed ground considerably over the last few years. At first it revolved around the persuasiveness or otherwise of impassioned readings of his films to reveal themes and psychology of such depth that Hitchcock should be talked of as an artist in the same breath as Dickens and Dostoevsky. This provoked lively debate, and unquestionably not only upgraded Hitchcock's reputation but that of Hollywood cinema and also that of film as an art form. As evidence of that, one need only point to the changing reputation over the years of **Vertigo**. A critical and commercial failure on its release in 1958, it is now, according to the most recent poll of international critics published in the magazine *Sight and Sound*, regarded as one of the dozen best films ever made.

Exercises in seeing

In recent years, though, the emphasis has been less on *what* Hitchcock's films communicate than on *how* they communicate. What does **Rear Window** tell us about the activity of watching films? How does Hitchcock succeed, in his words, in "playing the audience like an organ" in **Psycho**? Perhaps the way to approach Hitchcock, the argument goes, is to think of his films not as being art or about life but as exercises in *seeing*.

More than any other director, Hitchcock explicitly exploited the voyeur in every one of us, but he also demonstrated the deceptiveness of visual appearances. Nothing is as it seems in Hitchcock. James Stewart's noble exterior in **Vertigo** actually conceals a necrophile, while Tippi Hedren's immaculate appearance in **Marnie** (1964) is a facade that hides kleptomania and frigidity. Equally Hitchcock demonstrated that nowhere is safe – from the United Nations building to a motel shower. Hitchcock has made us alert to the potentially murderous in the most mundane or monumental settings, and his contribution to universal paranoia has undoubtedly been immense.

Film historians, rather than theorists, would define Hitchcock's importance from the standpoint of his technical innovations and experiments – his trailblazing use of sound in **Blackmail** (1929), the ten-minute take experiment in **Rope** (1948), his venture into special effects in **The Birds**.

One might add to this his significance as a trendsetter in the cinema (**Psycho** is indisputably the mother of the modern horror film) and the thematic as well as stylistic boldness of his work. In **Spellbound** (1945) and **Marnie**, he was not afraid to attempt a union between Freud and film, and few directors have made films that are more intensely dreamlike than Hitchcock's.

Shadow self

Recent biographers, notably the excellent Donald Spoto, have implied that his films might well stand as a representation of Hitchcock's own dreams and shadow self. Certainly one does not need to be a psychologist to sense that films of such eroticism, violence and disturbing visual imagery might well serve as a release for emotions or fantasies that in his own life the artist apparently found difficulty in expressing.

How revealing are the films about Hitchcock the man? It would be difficult to answer that about a man who, by his own admission, led an intensely orderly and private life. But to take one aspect of his personality: his sense of humor. Humor always had a wide-ranging function in his work. It reflected his reputation as a droll practical joker and fitted his conception of the cinema as "not a slice of life but a slice of cake". It reflected his love of counterpoint in his films, the sense that something deadly serious can look comically absurd when viewed from a different angle. It also was part of Hitchcock's quirky view of character, his sense that everyone had his or her own little obsessions and that nobody was quite normal. Fundamentally, it was a mark of his sanity and stability. **Strangers on a Train** (1951) and **Psycho** might be desolating portraits of human nature, but somehow Hitchcock's funfair antics in both films ensure that we are exhilarated rather than depressed by that disturbing exposure.

Defying conventions

Hitchcock's humor was also a mask. It kept interviewers off-balance and at arm's length, and it gave a sense of proportion to his occasional outrageousness. Yet, from time to time, a more intense and serious Hitchcock emerged. **I Confess** (1953) and **The Wrong Man** (1957) are religious films, whilst **Vertigo** is a Wagnerian song of love and death.

Hitchcock could often seem more pessimistic than playful, and the originality of his thrillers might lie less in their method or their manner than in their misanthropic morality. They defy conventional attitudes to good and evil, crime and punishment, and even on occasion a conventional attitude to narrative structure. Hitchcock despised whodunnits, partly because of their mechanical mystery plotting but also, one suspects, because of the moral complacency implied by the characterization of the master detective.

Hitchcock was terrified of the police, who are invariably stupid and harmful in his films, and who are always arresting the wrong people. With few exceptions, he contrives happy endings in which normality is restored, but the sheer devitalized nature of that normality might well have caused the crimes in the first place. His heart responds to lost souls like Uncle Charlie in **Shadow of a Doubt** (1943), Bruno in **Strangers on a Train** and Norman Bates in **Psycho**, who lash out frustratedly at the cages of family and society.

Psycho II (1983).

▲ *Meg Tilly takes a shower in Richard Franklin's sequel. Franklin is a great admirer of Hitchcock. His previous film thriller, **Roadgames** (1981), had a character called "Hitch" played by Jamie Lee Curtis, daughter of **Psycho** star Janet Leigh.*

◄ *A reappearance of mother's house in **Psycho II**. Norman Bates (Anthony Perkins) has now returned to it after twenty years, but is his mother really dead? And was she really his mother?*

His movies assert the ultimate triumph of good, but their fascination comes from their demonstration of the power of evil. They may conclude with the restoration of stability to relationships and society, but they dramatize the precariousness of that stability. The subject and resolutions of his movies might seem to encourage complacency, but everything about the *method* of them is designed to undermine any such complacency, to take you by surprise, to catch you out.

Obsession (1976).
◀ *Geneviève Bujold in Brian De Palma's thriller about a man who has unintentionally caused the death of his loved wife and who later comes across her double while she is carrying out restoration work in Florence cathedral. When* **Vertigo** *became unavailable for public screening for a number of years owing to a protracted legal dispute over copyright,* **Obsession** *became, in a sense, its double, an attempted restoration of a lost masterpiece.*

▼ *Falling in love again: Cliff Robertson embraces the double of his dead wife (Geneviève Bujold,), not knowing she is actually his daughter, bent on revenge. Contributing to the film's evocation of* **Vertigo** *is its circling camerawork at moments of high drama; its use in the narrative of dreams, paintings, letters and the church; and a thunderously romantic score from Hitchcock's most favored composer, Bernard Herrmann — one of his last and grandest compositions and itself a nostalgic homage to his Hitchcock years.*

Whether Hitchcock ever thought of his movies in those terms is open to question. But it might be that their power comes precisely from the fact that he was working at an instinctual level, not a conscious or calculated one. Because of this, the films retain a primal, subterranean force and continue to yield many meanings, not just one fixed interpretation.

Hitchcock always attempted to head off earnest discussion of his characters and ideas. "It's only a movie," he would say. Well, perhaps. But to those of us for whom movies are important – culturally, sociologically, aesthetically, or for pure escapism – Sir Alfred Hitchcock was, and remains, a giant.

▼ *Geneviève Bujold as the mother in a flashback scene. As in* **Vertigo***, the flashback is introduced very abruptly to explain what really happened in the kidnapping tragedy, events which the hero still has to piece together for himself.*

APPENDIX

Below is a list of Hitchcock's films as director, with release dates and principal actors

THE PLEASURE GARDEN (Germany) *1925 (released 1927)*

Virginia Valli, Carmelita Geraghty, Miles Mander, John Stuart

THE MOUNTAIN EAGLE (Germany) (USA: FEAR O' GOD) *1926 (released 1927)*

Nita Naldi, Bernard Goetzke, Malcolm Keen

THE LODGER: A STORY OF THE LONDON FOG *1926 (released 1927)*

Ivor Novello, June (sic), Malcolm Keen

DOWNHILL (USA: WHEN BOYS LEAVE HOME) *1927*

Ivor Novello, Isabel Jeans, Ian Hunter

EASY VIRTUE *1927*

Isabel Jeans, Robin Irvine, Violet Farebrother

THE RING *1927*

Carl Brisson, Ian Hunter, Lillian Hall Davis, Gordon Harker

THE FARMER'S WIFE *1928*

Lillian Hall Davis, Jameson Thomas

CHAMPAGNE *1928*

Betty Balfour, Jean Bradin, Gordon Harker

THE MANXMAN *1929*

Carl Brisson, Anny Ondra, Malcolm Keen

BLACKMAIL *1929*

Anny Ondra, John Longden, Donald Calthrop, Cyril Ritchard, Sara Allgood

JUNO AND THE PAYCOCK *1930*

Sara Allgood, Maire O'Neill, Sidney Morgan, Edward Chapman

MURDER! *1930*

Herbert Marshall, Norah Baring, Esme Percy, Miles Mander

THE SKIN GAME *1931*

Edmund Gwenn, John Longden, Jill Esmond, C. V. France

NUMBER SEVENTEEN *1932*

Leon M. Lion, Anne Grey, John Stuart

RICH AND STRANGE (USA: EAST OF SHANGHAI) *1932*

Henry Kendall, Joan Barry, Percy Marmont, Betty Amann, Elsie Randolph

WALTZES FROM VIENNA (USA: STRAUSS'S GREAT WALTZ) *1933*

Jessie Matthews, Esmond Knight, Fay Compton, Edmund Gwenn

THE MAN WHO KNEW TOO MUCH *1934*

Leslie Banks, Edna Best, Peter Lorre, Nova Pilbeam, Pierre Fresnay

THE 39 STEPS *1935*

Robert Donat, Madeleine Carroll, Godfrey Tearle, Lucie Mannheim, Peggy Ashcroft, John Laurie, Wylie Watson

SECRET AGENT *1936*

John Gielgud, Madeleine Carroll, Robert Young, Peter Lorre

SABOTAGE (USA: THE WOMAN ALONE) *1936*

Oscar Homolka, Sylvia Sidney, John Loder, Desmond Tester, Joyce Barbour

YOUNG AND INNOCENT (USA: THE GIRL WAS YOUNG) *1938*

Nova Pilbeam, Derrick de Marney, Mary Clare, Basil Radford

THE LADY VANISHES *1938*

Margaret Lockwood, Michael Redgrave, Dame May Witty, Paul Lukas, Naunton Wayne, Basil Radford

JAMAICA INN *1939*

Charles Laughton, Maureen O'Hara, Leslie Banks, Robert Newton

▲ Hitchcock making one of his earliest appearances in his film **Blackmail** (1929), hanging onto his hat while being pestered by a small boy (center frame). Seated to the right of Hitchcock is John Longden as the policeman who discovers that the murder he is investigating was committed by his girlfriend.

▲ A different angle on Cary Grant's walk up the stairs in **Suspicion**, (1941), the glass of milk gleaming in the dark. The figure of Grant has been transformed from that on page 57 to a dark menacing image.

▲ Robert Walker, trance-like, inadvertently almost kills a party guest in **Strangers on a Train** (1951).

▲ Convicted of murder in **Frenzy** (1972), Blaney (Jon Finch) arranges a fall so that he can be transferred to a hospital and attempt an escape. As usual in Hitchcock, the police have arrested the wrong man. Blaney is planning to avenge himself on the real murderer.

HITCHCOCK IN HOLLYWOOD

REBECCA (Academy Award: Best Picture) *1940*

Joan Fontaine, Laurence Olivier, Judith Anderson, George Sanders, Florence Bates

FOREIGN CORRESPONDENT *1940*

Joel McCrea, Laraine Day, Herbert Marshall, Albert Basserman, George Sanders

MR AND MRS SMITH *1941*

Carole Lombard, Robert Montgomery, Gene Raymond

SUSPICION (Academy Award: Best Actress – Joan Fontaine) *1941*

Joan Fontaine, Cary Grant, Nigel Bruce, Cedric Hardwicke, Dame May Witty, Isabel Jeans

SABOTEUR *1942*

Robert Cummings, Priscilla Lane, Otto Kruger, Norman Lloyd

SHADOW OF A DOUBT *1943*

Joseph Cotten, Teresa Wright, Hume Cronyn, MacDonald Carey, Patricia Collinge, Henry Travers, Edna May Wonacott, Wallace Ford

LIFEBOAT *1944*

Tallulah Bankhead, Walter Slezak, William Bendix, Mary Anderson, Hume Cronyn

BON VOYAGE (GB; French-language short) *1944*

Molière Players, John Blythe

AVENTURE MALGACHE (GB; French-language short) *1944*

Molière Players

SPELLBOUND *1945*

Ingrid Bergman, Gregory Peck, Leo G. Carroll, Michael Chekhov

NOTORIOUS *1946*

Ingrid Bergman, Cary Grant, Claude Rains, Leopoldine Konstantin

THE PARADINE CASE *1947*

Gregory Peck, Alida Valli, Charles Laughton, Ann Todd, Louis Jourdan

ROPE (color) *1948*

James Stewart, John Dall, Farley Granger, Cedric Hardwicke

UNDER CAPRICORN (GB; color) *1949*

Ingrid Bergman, Joseph Cotten, Michael Wilding, Margaret Leighton

STAGE FRIGHT (GB) *1950*

Marlene Dietrich, Jane Wyman, Richard Todd

CELEBRITY AND ARTIST

STRANGERS ON A TRAIN *1951*

Robert Walker, Farley Granger, Ruth Roman, Patricia Hitchcock

I CONFESS *1953*

Montgomery Clift, Anne Baxter, O. E. Hasse

DIAL M FOR MURDER (color) *1954*

Ray Milland, Grace Kelly, Robert Cummings, John Williams

REAR WINDOW (color) *1954*

James Stewart, Grace Kelly, Raymond Burr, Thelma Ritter

TO CATCH A THIEF (color) *1955*

Cary Grant, Grace Kelly, Jessie Royce Landis, Brigitte Auber

THE TROUBLE WITH HARRY (color) *1955*

John Forsythe, Shirley MacLaine, Edmund Gwenn, Mildred Natwick

THE MAN WHO KNEW TOO MUCH (color) *1956*

James Stewart, Doris Day, Bernard Miles, Brenda de Banzie

THE WRONG MAN *1956*

Henry Fonda, Vera Miles, Anthony Quayle

MASTERPIECES

VERTIGO (color) *1958*

James Stewart, Kim Novak, Barbara Bel Geddes, Tom Helmore

NORTH BY NORTHWEST (color) *1959*

Cary Grant, Eva Marie Saint, James Mason, Jessie Royce Landis, Leo G. Carroll

PSYCHO *1960*	Anthony Perkins, Janet Leigh, Vera Miles, John Gavin, Martin Balsam
THE BIRDS (color) *1963*	Tippi Hedren, Rod Taylor, Jessica Tandy, Suzanne Pleshette, Veronica Cartwright
MARNIE (color) *1964*	Tippi Hedren, Sean Connery, Diane Baker, Louise Latham

FINAL FILMS

TORN CURTAIN (color) *1966*	Paul Newman, Julie Andrews, Lila Kedrova, Tamara Toumanova
TOPAZ (color) *1969*	Frederick Stafford, Karin Dor, John Vernon, Michel Piccoli, Philippe Noiret
FRENZY (GB; color) *1972*	Jon Finch, Barry Foster, Anna Massey, Alec McCowen, Barbara Leigh-Hunt
FAMILY PLOT (color) *1976*	Bruce Dern, Barbara Harris, William Devane, Karen Black, Cathleen Nesbitt

TELEVISION FILMS (as director)

All black and white, half-hour series episodes (except where otherwise stated)

BREAKDOWN *1955*	Joseph Cotten
REVENGE *1955*	Vera Miles, Ralph Meeker
THE CASE OF MR PELHAM *1955*	Tom Ewell
BACK FOR CHRISTMAS *1956*	John Williams
WET SATURDAY *1956*	John Williams, Cedric Hardwicke
MR BLANCHARD'S SECRET *1956*	Mary Scott, Robert Horton
ONE MORE MILE TO GO *1957*	David Wayne
FOUR O'CLOCK (one-hour) *1957*	E. G. Marshall, Nancy Kelly
THE PERFECT CRIME *1957*	Vincent Price, James Gregory
LAMB TO THE SLAUGHTER *1958*	Barbara Bel Geddes
DIP IN THE POOL *1958*	Keenan Wynn, Fay Wray
POISON *1958*	James Donald
BANQUO'S CHAIR *1959*	John Williams, Kenneth Haigh
ARTHUR *1959*	Laurence Harvey, Hazel Court
THE CRYSTAL TRENCH *1959*	James Donald, Patricia Owens
INCIDENT AT A CORNER (one-hour; color) *1960*	Vera Miles, George Peppard, Paul Hartman
MRS BIXBY AND THE COLONEL'S COAT *1960*	Les Tremayne, Audrey Meadows
THE HORSEPLAYER *1961*	Claude Rains
BANG! YOU'RE DEAD *1961*	Billy Mumy
I SAW THE WHOLE THING (one-hour) *1962*	John Forsythe, Kent Smith

INDEX